Energy Cluster Policies for Sustainable Industrial Transformation

Environmental changes and related public policies require an energy-focused sustainable industrial transformation (SIT) that reconciles economic, environmental, and social objectives. Local energy clusters are conducive to these transformative processes since they represent institutional structures that link key actors and factors in territorial communities to form niches for the green transition. However, SIT policies at the local level are in a nascent stage, and empirical evidence on these processes remains scarce. Furthermore, it is necessary to advance a conceptual background for SIT and identify the development conditions for territorial energy communities. In response to these theory- and policy-related challenges, this monograph aims to conceptualize the role of energy cluster policies in SIT using an institutional approach, as well as to identify the progress of the energy cluster policies and the development stages, drivers, and obstacles of local energy clusters. The author's empirical basis will be Polish energy clusters analyzed against international policies and experience in territorial energy communities.

This book provides unique value by developing an institutional analytical framework for energy cluster policies, identifying the conditions for the development of energy clusters, and proposing actionable policy recommendations in this area.

Marta Gancarczyk is full professor and head of the Department of Finance and International Economics at the Institute of Economics, Finance and Management, Jagiellonian University in Krakow, Poland. She holds her Ph.D. in management science from the University of Lodz, Poland; the Habilituated Ph.D. in economics from Cracow University of Economics, Poland; and the professor's title based on the recommendation from the Polish Council of Excellence.

Joanna Bohatkiewicz-Czaicka is an adjunct professor at the Institute of Economics, Finance and Management, Jagiellonian University in Krakow, Poland. She holds her Ph.D. in economics and finance from the Jagiellonian University, M.A. in management and economic consultancy, and B.A. in business administration.

Jacek Gancarczyk is an adjunct professor at the Institute of Entrepreneurship, Jagiellonian University in Krakow, Poland. His research and publication activities are focused on innovative ventures, entrepreneurship, industrial clusters, and small and medium-sized enterprises.

Damian Tomczyk is a Ph.D. student in economics and finance, the Doctoral School in the Social Sciences, Jagiellonian University in Krakow. He holds a master's degree in economics at the Institute of Economics, Finance and Management, Jagiellonian University in Krakow. His research activities focus on ecological economics, in particular, on the energy industry and renewable energy sources.

Routledge Open Business and Economics

Routledge Open Business and Economics provides a platform for the open access publication of monographs and edited collections across the full breadth of these disciplines including accounting, finance, management, marketing, and political economy. Reflecting our commitment to supporting open access publishing, this series provides a key repository for academic research in business and economics.

Books in the series are published via the Gold Open Access model and are therefore available for free download and re-use according to the terms of Creative Commons licence. They can be accessed via the Routledge and Taylor & Francis website, as well as third party discovery sites such as the Directory of OAPEN Library, Open Access Books, PMC Bookshelf, and Google Books.

Note that the other Business and Economics series at Routledge also all accept open access books for publication.

Open Innovation and Startups
Michał Bańka

Energy Cluster Policies for Sustainable Industrial Transformation
An Institutional Perspective
Marta Gancarczyk, Joanna Bohatkiewicz-Czaicka, Jacek Gancarczyk, and Damian Tomczyk

Digital Internationalisation of Firms
Strategies, Challenges and Legal Aspects
Edited by Marzanna K. Witek-Hajduk, Magda Górska Grginović, and Bartosz Targański

For more information about this series, please visit: Routledge Open Business and Economics - Book Series - Routledge & CRC Press

Energy Cluster Policies for Sustainable Industrial Transformation

An Institutional Perspective

Marta Gancarczyk,
Joanna Bohatkiewicz-Czaicka,
Jacek Gancarczyk, and
Damian Tomczyk

NEW YORK AND LONDON

First published 2025
by Routledge
605 Third Avenue, New York, NY 10158

and by Routledge
4 Park Square, Milton Park, Abingdon, Oxon, OX14 4RN

Routledge is an imprint of the Taylor & Francis Group, an informa business

ISBN: 978-1-041-03369-1 (hbk)
ISBN: 978-1-041-03371-4 (pbk)
ISBN: 978-1-003-62354-0 (ebk)

DOI: 10.4324/9781003623540

Typeset in Times New Roman
by KnowledgeWorks Global Ltd.

Contents

List of Figures *vii*
List of Tables *viii*
Acknowledgments *ix*

Introduction 1

1 Clusters for Sustainable Industrial Transformation – The Institutional Approach 11

1.1 The Institutional Perspective on Sustainable Industrial Transformation 11
1.2 Clusters as Institutional Structures 15
1.3 The Role of Clusters and Institutions in Industrial Transitions 21
1.4 Institutional and Evolutionary Approach to Cluster Development 23

2 Energy Clusters in Multiscalar Energy Policy 36

2.1 The Essence and Legal Basis of Energy Clusters 36
2.2 Energy Clusters and Cluster-Based Policies 40
2.3 Local Energy Communities in Sustainable Development Policy 45
2.4 Institutional Framework for Energy Clusters in Poland 49

3 Research Framework and Methodological Approach to Evaluating Energy Cluster Policies 57

3.1 Research Framework 57
3.2 Methods, Data Sources, and Research Procedure 60
3.3 Operationalization and Measurement of the Research Framework Variables 66
3.4 Characteristics of the Research Sample 73

4 Sustainable Industrial Transformation in Polish Energy Clusters in the Context of International Cluster Policies 81

4.1 Development Phase of Polish Energy Clusters – Research Findings 81
4.2 Recommendations for Economic Policy in the Context of the International Energy Cluster Experience 98
4.3 Discussion of the Results and Synthesis 105
4.4 Contribution, Limitations, and Future Research Directions 107

Conclusion 113

Index 118

Figures

3.1	A research framework for evaluating the advancement of policies for ESIT through cluster initiatives	59
4.1	Scree plot with eigenvalues for determining the number of groups in the k-means analysis	82
4.2	Plot of means for two groups of energy clusters; standardized values	90
4.3	Legal conditions evaluated by energy cluster initiatives in the intermediate phase	95
4.4	Legal conditions evaluated by energy cluster initiatives in the birth phase	96

Tables

2.1 Legislation on energy clusters 39
2.2 Contribution of energy clusters to individual dimensions of sustainable development policy 48
2.3 Types of contracts applied by energy clusters 52
3.1 Methods and analytical techniques 61
3.2 Operationalization of the research framework variables 67
3.3 Measurement of the research framework variables 70
3.4 Scale reliability for the construct of cluster governance 72
3.5 Scale reliability for the construct of cluster energy-sustainable industrial transformation 72
3.6 Polish energy clusters resource and capability potential – a research sample characteristics 73
4.1 Analysis of variance in the sample researched 83
4.2 Group means for two development stages of energy cluster initiatives 84
4.3 Descriptive statistics of ESIT and governance indicators for two groups of clusters 85
4.4 The group means for resource and capability potential of the energy clusters 88
4.5 Euclidean distances between the groups of local energy clusters 89
4.6 Descriptive statistics for the resource and capability potential of the energy initiatives in the intermediate and birth phases 92
4.7 Economic barriers reported by energy cluster initiatives in different development phases 94
4.8 Legal conditions evaluated by energy cluster initiatives 95
4.9 Economic and legal drivers for energy clusters recommended by the respondents (paraphrases) 97

Acknowledgments

The authors would like to extend their sincere thanks to the anonymous reviewers of their book proposal to Routledge, who greatly supported them with both expertise and insightful evaluations. This research could not be disseminated without highly professional help, friendly advice, and excellent collaboration with Brianna Ascher, the Routledge editor of this monograph; Jessica Rech, editorial assistant at Routledge; and Zoe Everitt-Spence, editorial assistant at Routledge.

We gratefully acknowledge funding from the Priority Research Area "Society of the Future" under the Program "Excellence Initiative – Research University" at the Jagiellonian University in Krakow that enabled the publication of the book in an open access format.

This publication was written as part of "The green transition and economic polarization in Europe: a multi-level assessment with Germany and Poland as case studies" research project funded by the National Science Centre Poland (grant no. 2021/43/I/HS5/00538) and German Research Foundation (grant no. 504890580).

Introduction

Background and Research Problem

The great challenges of the environmental crisis and related public policies demand sustainable industrial transformation (SIT) based on energy; that is, a change in industrial structure, which not only addresses economic objectives, but reconciles efficiency with environmental and social goals (Grillitsch, 2015; Hassink et al., 2019; Luken & Castellanos-Silveria, 2011; Oinas et al., 2018; Trejo-Nieto, 2021). Clusters, including energy clusters, play a central role in driving industrial transformation by initiating economic changes or efficiently adapting to them (De Marchi et al., 2017; Jankowska & Götz, 2017; Zhan et al., 2020). The policy areas addressed with cluster initiatives include, among others, regional innovation policies, smart specialization strategies, and the advancement of Industries 4.0. and 5.0 (Foray, 2015; Gancarczyk & Konopa, 2021; Gancarczyk et al., 2021; Götz, 2020, 2021). Consequently, energy clusters are recognized in the economics of sustainable development as measures of policy in this area (Çağlar & Gürler, 2022). They can not only locally organize dispersed supply-demand transactions with a focus on renewable energy but also enhance social trust and consensus in communities facing high transition costs and institutional specifics (Mączyńska et al., 2024; Tomala & Urbaniec, 2024).

Key aspects include fostering SIT through place-based policies targeting European Union (EU)-wide goals and unique local conditions. Policies are necessary to achieve the low-carbon economy objectives, the European Green Deal, and service-oriented economies with high value-added activities. Public policies should recognize social well-being and inclusivity during transitions; optimize resource allocation; and secure public funding for digital transformation, defense, and social sector investments. These challenges are significant for policymakers, communities, enterprises, and academia in unstable settings (Speck et al., 2023; Trejo-Nieto, 2021; UNFCCC, 2023; United Nations, 2024).

Clusters can be understood as the agglomerations of networked companies and other organizations, operating in one or adjacent industries and forming

DOI: 10.4324/9781003623540-1

relationships with other organizations in the business environment (Bohatkiewicz & Gancarczyk, 2018; Bohatkiewicz-Czaicka & Gancarczyk, 2024, 2025; European Commission, 2002; Gancarczyk, 2010, 2015; Porter, 1998, 2000). However, the conceptualization of a cluster employed throughout our book is consistent with the term *cluster initiative*, an idea adopted in economic policy. It retains numerous characteristics of clusters, such as spatial proximity, industrial specialization, and network linkages. Nonetheless, it is free of industrial spatial concentration and the requisite critical mass of entities (Delgado et al., 2016; Sölvell et al., 2003).

Cluster initiatives differ in their internal structures, types of external linkages, stages of development, as well as value chain (VC) positions, and capability to advance in VCs (Bohatkiewicz-Czaicka & Gancarczyk, 2024, 2025; Gancarczyk, 2015; Trippl et al., 2015). According to the latest amendment to the Act of February 20, 2015 on Renewable Energy Sources, active from January 1, 2024, in Polish law, the energy cluster is defined as a cooperation agreement in the area of a generation, storage, demand balancing, distribution, or sale of electricity or fuels or heat, in order to provide economic, social, or environmental benefits to the parties or to increase the flexibility of the electricity system, whereby the parties in this agreement include at least a local government unit, or a capital company owned by a local government, or a capital company holding at least 50% of shares in a local government's company (Polish Journal of Laws of 2024, item 1361; Food and Agriculture Organization of the United Nations, 2015). Energy clusters are vital for the energy industry transformation. At the same time, policies for this transformation must align with technological progress and adhere to EU and international regulations (Berbeka, 2024; Engwerth et al., 2024).

Institutional analysis, recently acknowledged again by the Nobel Prize Awards, provides an in-depth understanding of socioeconomic behaviors influenced by formal and informal institutions (rules, norms, principles, regulations, and policies) (Helmke & Levitsky, 2004; North, 2010; Ostrom, 2010; Williamson, 2000). This institutional impact can be considered at three levels of O.E. Williamson's analysis (2000). The first level consists of customs, values, path-dependent rules of conduct, and the dominant logic in an industry (Hodgson, 2015; North, 2008; Ostrom, 2010). The second includes legal regulations and political systems that frame the formation and development of the energy clusters (Williamson, 2000). The third level embraces the governance which affects the functioning of a particular system, such as a cluster or territorial community (Colombelli et al., 2019; Helmke & Levitsky, 2004; Williamson, 2000; Zukauskaite et al., 2017). Governance represents internal sets of rules, such as the level of collaboration, methods to reconcile the interests of various stakeholders, and ways to set goals and development directions (Colombelli et al., 2019; Williamson, 2000).

Consequently, governance is context-dependent and legal and policy directions should be tailored to the development stages of cluster initiatives that differ in capabilities and support needs (Dragan, 2020; Jasiński et al., 2021; Mataczyńska & Kucharska, 2020; Sołtysik & Kozakiewicz, 2018; Surwillo, 2022; Tauron Polska Energia, 2024).

Research Gaps, Aim, and the Contribution

This monograph aims to conceptualize the role of energy cluster policies in SIT using an institutional approach, as well as to identify the progress of the energy cluster policies and the development stages, drivers and obstacles of local energy clusters. We use Polish energy clusters as our empirical basis, and our conceptual foundation will be institutional and coevolutionary perspective. *The general argument of the book* is that the processes and effects of energy-sustainable industrial transformation (ESIT) through cluster initiatives can be identified and explained by acknowledging institutional aspects, including socioeconomic governance within cluster initiatives, legal arrangements and multiscalar policy interventions.

This monograph will address three research and policy gaps. *First, there is a scarcity of research enhancing the design of place-based policies adjusted to various transition contexts* (Coenen & Truffer, 2012; Luken & Castellanos-Silveria, 2011; Smith et al., 2004). Industrial transformation processes are increasingly pivotal to the formulation and execution of public policies at the global, national, regional and local levels (Ashford et al., 2002; Chembessi et al., 2024; Coenen & Truffer, 2012; Schwabe, 2024). Locally, energy clusters are crucial to promoting green transitions by supporting sustainable socioeconomic frameworks and the adoption of renewable energy. They provide a bottom-up method to create and expand replicable niches to larger areas (Bohatkiewicz-Czaicka & Gancarczyk, 2025). This is particularly significant in countries like Poland, where energy-intensive industries necessitate substantial shifts toward renewable energy sources (Micek et al., 2021; Surwillo, 2022; Campos-Romero et al., 2024) and cluster-based policies are still in the developmental phases (Dragan, 2020; Grigore & Dragan, 2020).

Second, a conceptual background for energy-focused SIT is needed and to identify the policy arrangements that favor or impede this transition (Bohatkiewicz-Czaicka & Gancarczyk, 2025; Micek et al., 2021; Surwillo, 2022). The interrelated concepts of energy clusters and SIT constitute a significant theoretical framework for elucidating energy transition, thus conceiving the notion of ESIT (Ashford et al., 2002; Grigore & Dragan, 2020; Smith et al., 2004). These essential constructs have been isolated in academic discourse, overlooking the holistic potential. An institutional perspective is suitable to highlight industrial change in complex territorial contexts. Few studies (Luken & Castellanos-Silveria, 2011; Smith et al., 2004; Speck et al., 2023; Trejo-Nieto, 2021) address socioeconomic governance in SIT and ESIT.

Third, the literature on energy clusters and policies is in the exploratory stage and predominantly includes qualitative case studies (Afeltowicz et al., 2024; Micek et al., 2021; Surwillo, 2022). This highlights the importance of a detailed exploration of specific phenomena. However, synthesis and generalization are crucial to understanding the current state and guiding future research, aiding both science and practical use (Meshkov, 2019). Consequently, larger samples are needed to provide evidence from which generalizations and policy recommendations can be derived.

Based on the conceptual background and research gaps, we formulate the research questions:

RQ1. What is the advancement of energy cluster policies in Poland considering a multiscalar context at the local, country, and international levels?
RQ2. What are the development phases of the energy cluster initiatives in Poland?
RQ3. What are the barriers and drivers of energy cluster initiatives in Poland?
RQ4. What are the recommendations for energy cluster policies to enhance sustainable industrial transformation?

The responses to the research questions yielded a range of insights and practical implications; hence, our research provides *theoretical and practical contributions. This study enhances theory on clusters and sustainable industrial transformation.* The monograph provides a framework for cluster policies with an institutional and coevolutionary perspective (Markusen, 2004; Martin & Sunley, 2007). It categorizes energy clusters in Poland by characteristics and stages, serving as a model for ESIT progression in other countries. It identifies drivers and obstacles in initial cluster initiatives, enhancing industrial transformation knowledge. Using a deductive mixed-method approach, our research enables broader generalization compared to the existing case-based investigations on energy clusters and communities.

This research makes significant contributions to economic policy. The monograph's value lies in policy recommendations based on theoretical and empirical evidence. It synthesizes multilevel policies affecting energy clusters and industrial transformation. Moreover, it identifies barriers and drivers of cluster development which are informative for cluster administration and policymakers. The findings support the design of policy for energy cluster initiatives, highlighting the need to integrate these activities into regional, national, and international energy systems and socioeconomic frameworks. Secondly, our findings significantly contribute by outlining prerequisites for a local-level green transition, crucial for place-based policies. These measures are expected to form replicable local energy communities for distributed resources and grid, enhancing resource management and resilience. Moreover, the findings and recommendations can potentially be applied to other industries, accounting for their unique technological and spatial traits.

The Method

In the theoretical part of the monograph, we adopt the method of *narrative literature review*. The review covered theoretical literature and empirical studies in industrial policy, clusters and cluster evolution, regional industrial transformation, and SIT as well as institutional and coevolutionary approaches in economics and economic geography.

In the empirical part, to verify the research framework and understand the empirical evidence, we used a mixed-method approach, which included secondary source analysis and surveys among Polish energy clusters initiatives, supplemented by semi-structured interviews with clusters' administration. Due to the numerous variables and small sample size, we applied descriptive statistics, exploratory data analysis like principal component analysis, and cluster taxonomical analysis. We used k-means clustering to identify cluster configurations related to development phases and profiles. Additionally, we performed qualitative content analysis of interview insights and secondary data analysis of reports, past research on energy clusters, and energy policy evaluations.

Findings

The research successfully achieved its objectives by advancing the study of early industrial transformation, focusing on energy clusters. It advanced the conceptual framework of SIT using energy clusters as empirical basis and integrating institutional and coevolutionary approaches.

The study provided a comprehensive description of the progression of energy cluster policies across local, national and international scales. Moreover, the research identified the development phases of the energy cluster initiatives in a country context (Martin & Sunley, 2007). Our findings revealed limited progress in energy cluster policies, categorizing these initiatives at an initial stage of development. Furthermore, our research elucidated the obstacles and motivating factors that impact the energy cluster initiatives. The major obstacles include a relatively minor proportion of renewable energy in the overall energy supply of clusters, insufficient innovation levels, and low participant density. Ultimately, recommendations were articulated to inform energy cluster policies aimed at fostering ESIT.

The Structure of the Monograph

This monograph includes four chapters, an introduction, and a conclusion. *The first chapter* examines industrial transformation, providing definitions and emphasizing aspects like regional and sustainable transformation. It explains clusters as institutional structures, detailing their structural characteristics, and discusses the role of clusters and institutions in local transformation through institutional and coevolutionary perspectives.

The second chapter outlines national and European legislation for energy clusters in Poland, defines energy clusters, and reviews regulations for the Polish energy sector. It presents policies for energy clusters, highlighting their role in achieving sustainable development goals. The chapter also details institutions providing support, financing, and governance for these clusters and concludes with an evaluation of their development in Poland.

The third chapter describes a research framework and methodological approach to evaluate energy cluster development. It guides the empirical study of Polish energy cluster initiatives as policy tools, focusing on their development phase, barriers, drivers of their advancement, and the country's distributed energy transformation context. The framework highlights key theoretical connections, followed by research methods and procedures for evaluation. This chapter also presents research findings, detailing Polish energy clusters' context and research sample attributes.

The fourth chapter presents research findings on SIT in Polish energy clusters, including a discussion and contribution explanation. We compare empirical results with international research on energy clusters and sustainable industrial policies. Additionally, we offer business and economic policy recommendations. The explanation of theoretical and practical contributions, limitations, and future research directions summarize the chapter.

The concluding section explains how the main objective was accomplished in this monograph. Furthermore, this section synthesizes the content of the monograph and provides the major outcomes and recommendations.

References

Food and Agriculture Organization of the United Nations (2015). *Act on renewable energy sources* (amended in 2024; Polish Journal of Laws of 2024, item 1361). https://www.fao.org/faolex/results/details/en/c/LEX-FAOC151966/

Afeltowicz, Ł., Nawojczyk, M., & Tyrała, R. (2024). Entrepreneurial actions in energy transition: A study of three local energy clusters in Poland. *European Urban and Regional Studies, 31*(2), 132–148. https://doi.org/10.1177/09697764231179667

Ashford, N. A., Hafkamp, W., Prakke, F., & Vergragt, P. (2007). *Pathways to Sustainable Industrial Transformations: Co-optimising Competitiveness, Employment, and Environment.*

Berbeka, K. (2024). *Integracja europejska: Wybrane aspekty ekonomiczne i środowiskowe* (Wydanie I). Wydawnictwo Uniwersytetu Jagiellońskiego. https://doi.org/10.4467/K7569.123/23.24.19388

Bohatkiewicz, J., & Gancarczyk, M. (2018). *Structural characteristics of industrial clusters: The essence and measurement.* Wyższa Szkoła Biznesu-National-Louis University. https://ruj.uj.edu.pl/xmlui/handle/item/57094

Bohatkiewicz-Czaicka, J., & Gancarczyk, M. (2024). *Ewolucja koncepcji klastrów a uwarunkowania ich globalnej pozycji.* Wydawnictwo UJ.

Bohatkiewicz-Czaicka, J., & Gancarczyk, M. (2025). *Industrial clusters in international value chains: Conceptual advancement and empirical evidence from European ICT clusters*. Taylor & Francis.

Çağlar, M., & Gürler, C. (2022). Sustainable Development Goals: A cluster analysis of worldwide countries. *Environment, Development and Sustainability*, *24*(6), 8593–8624. https://doi.org/10.1007/s10668-021-01801-6

Campos-Romero, H., Rodil-Marzábal, Ó., & Gómez Pérez, A. L. (2024). Environmental asymmetries in global value chains: The case of the European automotive sector. *Journal of Cleaner Production*, *449*, 141606. https://doi.org/10.1016/j.jclepro.2024.141606

Chembessi, C., Bourdin, S., & Torre, A. (2024). Towards a territorialisation of the circular economy: The proximity of stakeholders and resources matters. *Cambridge Journal of Regions, Economy and Society*, *rsae007*.

Coenen, L., & Truffer, B. (2012). Places and spaces of sustainability transitions: Geographical contributions to an emerging research and policy field. *European Planning Studies*, *20*(3), 367–374.

Colombelli, A., Paolucci, E., & Ughetto, E. (2019). Hierarchical and relational governance and the life cycle of entrepreneurial ecosystems. *Small Business Economics*, *52*, 505–521.

Delgado, M., Porter, M. E., & Stern, S. (2016). Defining clusters of related industries. *Journal of Economic Geography*, *16*(1), 1–38. https://doi.org/10.1093/jeg/lbv017

De Marchi, V., Gereffi, G., & Grandinetti, R. (2017). Evolutionary trajectories of industrial districts in global value chains. In V. De Marchi, E. Di Maria, & G. Gereffi (Eds.), *Local clusters in global value chains: Linking actors and territories through manufacturing and innovation* (pp. 33–50). Routledge. https://doi.org/10.4324/9781315182049

Dragan, D. (2020). Legal barriers to the development of energy clusters in Poland. *European Energy and Environmental Law Review*, *29*(1), 14–20.

Engwerth, V., Kigle, S., Ruprecht, D., Mohr, S., & Guminski, A. (2024). Modeling transformation pathways of European final energy consumption in the transport and buildings sector using country clustering. *Energy Technology*, *13*(2), 14–20. https://doi.org/10.1002/ente.202300951

European Commission (2002). *Regional clusters in Europe. Observatory of European SMEs* (Vol. 2). Office for Official Publications of the European Communities.

Foray, D. (2015). Should we let the genie out of the bottle? On the new industrial policy agenda and the example of smart specialisation. In R. Antonietti, F. Gambarotto, & G. Coro (Eds.), *Uscire dalla crisi: Città, comunità, specializzazioni intelligenti* (pp. 25–28). Franco Angeli.

Gancarczyk, M. (2010). Model schyłku i odrodzenia klastrów. *Gospodarka Narodowa*, *3*, 1–21.

Gancarczyk, M. (2015). Enterprise- and industry-level drivers of cluster evolution and their outcomes for clusters from developed and less-developed countries. *European Planning Studies*, *23*(10), 1932–1952. https://doi.org/10.1080/09654313.2014.959811

Gancarczyk, M., & Konopa, S. (2021). Exploring the governance of entrepreneurial ecosystems for productive high growth. *Foresight and STI Governance*, *15*(4), 9–21. https://doi.org/10.17323/2500-2597.2021.4.9.21

Gancarczyk, M., Ujwary-Gil, A., & González-López, M. (2021). *Partnerships for regional innovation and development*. Routledge.

Götz, M. (2020). Cluster role in Industry 4.0 – A pilot study from Germany. *Competitiveness Review: An International Business Journal, 31*(1), 54–82.

Götz, M. (2021). *Clusters, digital transformation and regional development in Germany*. Routledge.

Grigore, A. M., & Dragan, I. M. (2020). Towards sustainable entrepreneurial ecosystems in a transitional economy: An analysis of two Romanian city-regions through the lens of entrepreneurs. *Sustainability (Switzerland), 12*(15), 6061. https://doi.org/10.3390/su12156061

Grillitsch, M. (2015). Institutional layers, connectedness and change: Implications for economic evolution in regions. *European Planning Studies, 23*(10), 2099–2124. https://doi.org/10.1080/09654313.2014.1003796

Hassink, R., Isaksen, A., & Trippl, M. (2019). Towards a comprehensive understanding of new regional industrial path development. *Regional Studies, 53*(11), 1636–1645. https://doi.org/10.1080/00343404.2019.1566704

Helmke, G., & Levitsky, S. (2004). Informal institutions and comparative politics: A research agenda. *Perspectives on Politics, 2*(4), 725–740.

Hodgson, G. M. (2015). On defining institutions: Rules versus equilibria. *Journal of Institutional Economics, 11*(3), 497–505. https://doi.org/10.1017/S1744137415000028

Jankowska, B., & Götz, M. (2017). Internationalization intensity of clusters and their impact on firm internationalization: The case of Poland. *European Planning Studies, 25*(6), 958–977. https://doi.org/10.1080/09654313.2017.1296111

Jasiński, J., Kozakiewicz, M., & Sołtysik, M. (2021). Determinants of energy cooperatives' development in rural areas—Evidence from Poland. *Energies, 14*(2), 319. https://doi.org/10.3390/en14020319

Mataczyńska, E., & Kucharska, A., Eds. (2020). *Klastry energii: Regulacje, teoria i praktyka*. Wydawnictwo Naukowe Instytutu Polityki Energetycznej im. I. Łukasiewicza. https://www.instytutpe.pl/wp-content/uploads/2019/09/Klastry-energii.-Regulacje-teoria-i-praktyka.pdf

Luken, R., & Castellanos-Silveria, F. (2011). Industrial transformation and sustainable development in developing countries. *Sustainable Development, 19*(3), 167–175.

Mączyńska, E., Pysz, P., & Urbaniec, M. (2024). Społeczna Gospodarka Rynkowa w dobie transformacji energetycznej w Unii Europejskiej i Ukrainie. In E. Mączyńska, P. Pysz, & M. Urbaniec (Eds.), *Polskie Towarzystwo Ekonomiczne Oddział w Poznaniu*. https://doi.org/10.52335/9788365269478

Markusen, A. (2004). Sticky places in slippery space: A typology of industrial districts. *Economic Geography, 72*(3), 293–313.

Martin, R., & Sunley, P. (2007). Complexity thinking and evolutionary economic geography. *Journal of Economic Geography, 7*(5), 573–601. https://doi.org/10.1093/jeg/lbm019

Meshkov, I. (2019). Analysis of cluster initiatives in the energy sector of the EU. In V. Litvinenko (Ed.), *Youth technical sessions proceedings* (pp. 45–49). CRC Press. https://doi.org/10.1201/9780429327070-7

Micek, D., Kocór, M., Worek, B., & Szczucka, A. (2021). *Społeczne uwarunkowania funkcjonowania klastrów energii w Polsce: Raport podsumowujący analizę studium przypadku wybranych klastrów: Cz. 3*. Ministerstwo Rozwoju, Pracy i Technologii, Akademia Górniczo-Hutnicza im. Stanisława Staszica w Krakowie, Narodowe Centrum Badań Jądrowych. https://www.er.agh.edu.pl/media/filer_public/66/cb/66cb3fd2-854d-47c5-baaa-c2952fb8e639/raport_spoleczne_uwarunkowania_funkcjonowania_klastrow_energii_w_polsce.pdf

North, D. C. (2008). Institutions and the Performance of Economies over Time. In C. Ménard, & M. M. Shirley (Eds.), *Handbook of new institutional economics* (pp. 21–30). Springer. https://doi.org/10.1007/978-3-540-69305-5_2

North, D. C. (2010). *Understanding the process of economic change*. Princeton University Press.

Oinas, P., Trippl, M., & Höyssä, M. (2018). Regional industrial transformations in the interconnected global economy. *Cambridge Journal of Regions, Economy and Society, 11*(2), 227–240. https://doi.org/10.1093/cjres/rsy015

Ostrom, E. (2010). Beyond markets and states: Polycentric governance of complex economic systems. *American Economic Review, 100*(3), 641–672.

Porter, M. E. (1998). Clusters and the new economics of competition. *Harvard Business Review, 76*(6), 77–90.

Porter, M. E. (2000). Location, competition, and economic development: Local clusters in a global economy. *Economic Development Quarterly, 14*(1), 15–34. https://doi.org/10.1177/089124240001400105

Raines, P. (Ed.) (2017). *Cluster development and policy*. Taylor and Francis.

Schwabe, J. (2024). Regime-driven niches and institutional entrepreneurs: Adding hydrogen to regional energy systems in Germany. *Energy Research & Social Science, 108*, 103357.

Smith, A., Stirling, A., & Berkhout, F. (2004). *Governing sustainable industrial transformation under different transition contexts*. In *Governance for Industrial Transformation, Proceedings of the 2003 Berlin Conference on the Human Dimensions of Global Environmental Change* (pp. 113–132). https://www.academia.edu/download/30715730/10.1.1.197.8530.pdf

Sołtysik, M., & Kozakiewicz, M. (2018). Selected optimization issues in the energy clusters. *Rynek Energii, 2018*(3), 9–14.

Sölvell, Ö., Lindqvist, G., & Ketels, C. H. M. (2003). *The cluster initiative greenbook*. Ivory Tower.

Speck, S., Paleari, S., Tagliapietra, S., & Zoboli, R. (2023). *Investments in the sustainability transition: Leveraging green industrial policy against emerging constraints*. EEA European Environment Agency. https://doi.org/10.2800/451268

Surwillo, I. (2022). Energy clusters in Poland: Towards diffused green energy communities. In F. Karimi, & M. Rodi (Eds.), *Energy transition in the Baltic Sea region* (pp. 185–204). Routledge.

Tauron Polska Energia (2024). *Energy Clusters in the activities of the Ministry of Energy*. https://www.tauron.pl/tauron/o-tauronie/tauron-dla-otoczenia/klastry-energii

Tomala, J., & Urbaniec, M. (2024). Towards sustainable development in the European Union: A critical raw materials perspective. *Economics and Environment, 88*(1), 654. https://doi.org/10.34659/eis.2024.88.1.654

Trejo-Nieto, A. (2021). Green industrial policies for sustainability and resilience. In R. Brears (Ed.), *The Palgrave encyclopedia of sustainable resources and ecosystem resilience* (pp. 1–18). Springer International Publishing. https://doi.org/10.1007/978-3-030-67776-3_33-1

Trippl, M., Grillitsch, M., Isaksen, A., & Sinozic, T. (2015). Perspectives on cluster evolution: Critical review and future research issues. *European Planning Studies, 23*(10), 2028–2044. https://doi.org/10.1080/09654313.2014.999450

UNFCCC (2023). *Leaving No One Behind in the Transition Towards a Low-Carbon Economy*. https://unfccc.int/news/leaving-no-one-behind-in-the-transition-towards-a-low-carbon-economy. Accessed December 25, 2024.

United Nations (2024). *The 17 Goals. The 2030 Agenda for Sustainable Development.* https://sdgs.un.org/goals

Williamson, O. E. (2000). The new institutional economics: Taking stock, looking ahead. *Journal of Economic Literature*, *38*(3), 595–613.

Zhan, J., Bolwijn, R., Casella, B., & Santos-Paulino, A. (2020). Global value chain transformation to 2030: Overall direction and policy implications. *VoxEU & CEPR.*

Zukauskaite, E., Trippl, M., & Plechero, M. (2017). Institutional thickness revisited. *Economic Geography*, *93*(4), 325–345.

1 Clusters for Sustainable Industrial Transformation – The Institutional Approach

1.1 The Institutional Perspective on Sustainable Industrial Transformation

Institutional Foundations of Sustainable Industrial Transformation

Industrial transformation or industrial transition represents a profound change in industrial structure that can manifest as technological shifts, innovative products and processes replacing the obsolete ones, and new relationships between supply and demand to enhance competitiveness and build resilience (Hassink et al., 2019; Isaksen et al., 2019; Oinas et al., 2018; Wojnicka-Sycz et al., 2022). Sustainable industrial transformation (SIT) is an extension of the industrial transformation concept which not only addresses economic objectives but reconciles efficiency with environmental and social goals (Grillitsch, 2015; Hassink et al., 2019; Luken & Castellanos-Silveria, 2011; Manowska et al., 2017; Oinas et al., 2018; Trejo-Nieto, 2021). Consequently, energy-sustainable industrial transformation (ESIT) is a manifestation of SIT in a particular context of the energy industry. As a type of structural change, ESIT can be achieved through institutional and policy-driven solutions, such as energy cluster initiatives (Ashford et al., 2002; Elzen & Wieczorek, 2005; Grigore & Dragan, 2020; Jasiński et al., 2021; Mucha-Kuś et al., 2021; Smith et al., 2004). The institutional framework underscores the critical role of multilevel governance, collaborative innovation networks, and the influence of historical trajectories (path dependence) in driving and shaping regional industrial evolution. A spatial approach to industrial transformation is recognized due to its impact on specific territories and the mutual influence of territorial contexts in shaping the unique nature of industrial change (Grillitsch et al., 2018).

As a spatial phenomenon, SIT is intrinsically linked to industrial path development, drawing on evolutionary and coevolutionary economics, which emphasize adaptive processes and interdependencies among actors and systems over time (Gong & Hassink, 2019; Martin & Sunley, 2006). The literature on industrial transformation, cluster development, and energy clusters appears

DOI: 10.4324/9781003623540-2

fragmented and lacking a comprehensive, multiscalar approach that interconnects these phenomena. Energy clusters, being situated at the local level within these policies, can serve as pivotal instruments for constructing suitable environment for the occurrence of SIT. Therefore, it is essential to address the underexplored area of energy-focused SIT and elaborate a conceptual framework addressing this field (Bohatkiewicz-Czaicka & Gancarczyk, 2025; Micek et al., 2021; Surwillo, 2022).

Industrial Policies as an Integral Component of Institutional Perspective on SIT

The primary component of the institutional perspective that facilitates industrial transformation are industrial policies (Gancarczyk & Ujwary-Gil, 2020). Industrial policies can transform industries, as seen in the Małopolska region of Poland after joining the European Union in 2004. Innovation policy supported industrial change and created new opportunities in the referred region. Interactions between policy and industry were shaped by institutional mechanisms such as policy mix, stakeholder representation, and macroeconomic processes. These mechanisms balanced existing capabilities with exploring new economic areas, promoting new growth pathways. Understanding these mechanisms reveals how policies and industry evolve together, illustrating their dynamic relationship (Gancarczyk et al., 2023).

Policy formulation is transitioning from a top-down approach, which emphasizes nationwide and vertical focus on select industries or enterprise winners, to horizontal programs aimed at enhancing the general business environment, including competition protection, skill promotion, education, research and development (R&D), and infrastructure development (Bailey et al., 2019; Gancarczyk & Ujwary-Gil, 2020). The New Industrial Policy (NIP) introduces a transition toward place-based, micro-level, bottom-up methodologies, alongside collaborative partnerships, for the formulation and execution of policies (Aiginger & Rodrik, 2020; European Commission, 2020; Gancarczyk & Ujwary-Gil, 2020). NIP adopts a multiscalar approach, integrating top-down design with bottom-up implementation, involving regional, local governments and stakeholders. NIP's scope covers the entire economy, expanding industrial policy from manufacturing to services and the public sector (Aiginger & Rodrik, 2020). This is also a transition from purely technological and economic upgrading to responsible innovation and environmental protection (Aiginger & Rodrik, 2020; European Commission, 2020; Gancarczyk & Ujwary-Gil, 2020; Janssen & Frenken, 2019). The crucial conditions for NIP include research and regional innovation strategies (smart specialization), industrial transformation and upgrading in global value chains, the Fourth Industrial Revolution and Industry 4.0, entrepreneurial discovery, and sustainable ecological and digital transitions (Sycz & Wojnicka-Sycz, 2023).

The institutional framework that comes along with NIP involves national, regional, and local governments, as well as academia, business organizations, and other intermediary bodies (Gancarczyk & Ujwary-Gil, 2020). The main directions of NIP formulated in *New Industrial Strategy for Europe* (European Commission, 2020) include globally competitive industry, industrial transformation towards climate neutrality, and digitalization together with the enhancement of environmentally responsible industries while acknowledging societal expectations (Aiginger & Rodrik, 2020; Gancarczyk & Ujwary-Gil, 2020).

The Coevolutionary Approach to SIT

The spatial aspect in the institutional approach stems from coevolution, which offers valuable insights into regional industrial dynamics. It highlights reciprocal influences between entities, where one's evolution depends on another's trajectory, fostering codependent relationships. Integrating this concept into economics, especially industrial dynamics, regional economics, and economic geography, enhances understanding of sustainability-oriented transitions. Namely, it underscores the complexity inherent in industrial change, encompassing the interactions of various actors and factors within a geographic space and temporal framework (Gancarczyk et al., 2023; Gong & Hassink, 2019; Martin & Sunley, 2006).

An institutional approach combined with a coevolutionary perspective is grounded in the belief that the policies introduced interact with industrial transformation on the basis of a feedback loop, i.e., a two-way interaction relationship (Benner, 2022). On the one hand, the creation of new policies aims to improve the conditions for the emergence and development of industrial transformation. However, the industrial transition processes themselves force the emergence and changes in the applied policies. The transformations discerned among policymakers, individuals, or groups engaged with policies, and those operating within an industry, are tangible manifestations of the broader effects of coevolutionary processes (Benner, 2022; Frenken & Boschma, 2007; Gancarczyk et al., 2023).

The influence of industry on policy tends to be more dispersed, often channeled through interest groups, and shaped by the inclusiveness of policymaking processes and the capacity of enterprises to organize and advocate for their interests (Foray et al., 2012). These transformations illuminate the dynamic interplay between industrial and policy environments, leading to significant shifts across various domains. These outcomes may encompass changes in the social system and institutional framework, such as cooperation routines and conventions (Grillitsch, 2015; Zukauskaite et al., 2017). They also manifest themselves in industrial structures, such as the emergence or restructuring of industrial pathways or adjustments in policy trajectories that align with evolving development objectives and implementation strategies (Gancarczyk et al., 2023; Yeung, 2019).

The Relationship of Institutional and Coevolutionary Approaches in the Process of Industry Transformation towards SIT

The theoretical framework of institutional and coevolutionary approaches emphasizes how both policy adaptations and industrial advancements reciprocally shape each other, contributing to a dynamic environment where each agent informs and adjusts to the changes in the other. Furthermore, it integrates the concepts of regional and SIT as well as incorporates interaction mechanisms (Gancarczyk et al., 2023). These mechanisms define the interdependent roles that policy and industry play, providing insights into major trajectories in industrial development and guiding policy approaches. They are one of the means to explain coevolutionary structural changes. Interaction mechanisms are processes theoretically grounded in the concept of multiscalarity and focused on outcomes. These mechanisms shape the reciprocal influence between policy and industry, offering a framework for understanding their coevolution (Gancarczyk et al., 2023; Yeung, 2019). Multiscalarity, in turn, emphasizes the dynamics and processes emerging both from within coevolving populations and from their interactions with local, regional, national, and international contexts (Benner, 2022; Chen & Hassink, 2020; Gancarczyk et al., 2023; Gong & Hassink, 2020). The concept of multiscalarity reflects multilevel spatial influences and contextual specificity of the processes of territorial development (Benner, 2022; Chen & Hassink, 2020; Gong & Hassink, 2019, 2020; Yeung, 2019).

The theoretical framework of the coevolutionary perspective leading to industrial transformation is based on mechanisms of interaction which can be internally and externally driven and bear multiscalar character. In other words, industrial transformation is driven by a feedback loop of policies and industries, as well as exploitation and exploration processes in industrial development and policy directions (Gancarczyk et al., 2023; Gong & Hassink, 2019). This perspective improves the understanding of how policy and industry evolve together, with interaction mechanisms offering a structured lens for analyzing these reciprocal adaptations and their impact on regional economic progress.

Consequently, although industrial transformation processes are located in spatial proximity, they need to undergo multiscalar influences, including positioning within a global value chain. Value chain upgrading and industrial transformation require transformative technologies, such as environmental technologies related with renewable energy sources (RESs). These solutions not only protect the environment and improve the social and health condition but can enhance productivity and foster convergence toward novel industrial structures, including distributed, as opposed to centralized, energy systems, with energy clusters as one of the key actors (Ciffolilli & Muscio, 2018; Gancarczyk & Ujwary-Gil, 2020; Marhold, 2015).

1.2 Clusters as Institutional Structures

Exploring the Theoretical Framework of Clusters and Institutions as Basic Concepts for Research

Clusters as a concept and form of industrial organization represent geographically proximate concentrations of companies in the same or related, interconnected industries that form linkages with organizations and resources of the regional environment, such as specialized suppliers, service providers, and associated institutions, such as universities and research centers (Bohatkiewicz & Gancarczyk, 2018; Bohatkiewicz-Czaicka & Gancarczyk, 2024, 2025; European Commission, 2002; Gancarczyk, 2010, 2015; Porter, 1998). However, clusters have undergone a transformation from being perceived merely as simple agglomerations of specialized entities to being recognized as institutional frameworks that systematically coordinate resources and knowledge, while also implementing policies (Fornahl et al., 2015). *In the realm of economic policy, clusters are conceptualized as cluster initiatives.* This concept retains numerous characteristics of traditional clusters, such as agglomeration (spatial proximity), industry specialization, and network linkages. Nonetheless, it overlooks spatial concentration and the requisite critical mass, which is conventionally quantified by the location quotient (Delgado et al., 2016; Sölvell et al., 2003). It is crucial to underscore that this conceptualization of a cluster, as a cluster initiative, is the interpretation used throughout our book.

This evolutionary progression is particularly observable in the context of energy clusters (Bergal, 2020; Coenen et al., 2021; McCauley & Stephens, 2012; Sjøtun & Njøs, 2019). This evolutionary trajectory underscores their pivotal role in facilitating innovation, advancing regional economic development, and enhancing resilience to external perturbations through adaptable institutional frameworks (Hu & Hassink, 2020). Clusters, by serving as intermediaries between individual enterprises and macro-level policy frameworks, typify the synthesis of localized collaboration and institutional integration, thereby distinguishing themselves from organizational paradigms characterized by greater hierarchical structuring or dispersion (Lis et al., 2020). The concurrent functions of both regional and national institutions underscore the importance of employing a multiscalar approach in comprehending cluster dynamics and their integrated institutional frameworks (Andreoni et al., 2024; Ayrapetyan & Hermans, 2020).

Clusters as institutional structures assume a broad understanding of the institution as the rules of the game group (North, 1990); groups of stakeholders like enterprises, universities, research centers (Nelson, 1993); institutional setup as guidelines for activities (Lundvall, 1992); laws and customs (Veblen, 1919); and social rules (Hodgson, 2006; Lubacha & Wendler, 2021). Additional pertinent institutions encompass academia, business organizations, as well as clusters, technology parks, and various organizational forms dedicated to technology transfer and enterprise support (Asheim et al., 2019). Institutional analysis, which was recently acknowledged by the Nobel Prize Awards, provides a comprehensive understanding of social and economic behaviors influenced by both formal and informal institutions, construed not merely as rules, norms, or principles but also as regulations and policies (Helmke & Levitsky, 2004; North, 2010; Ostrom, 2010; Williamson, 2000). The institutional impact may be evaluated according to the tripartite framework posited by O. E. Williamson in his analysis (2000). Specifically, the first level encompasses informal institutions, which include customs, values, path-dependent rules of conduct, and the prevailing logic within an industry (Hodgson, 2015; North, 2008; Ostrom, 2010). The tier of formal institutions encompasses statutory regulations and political frameworks that delineate the manner in which energy clusters are constituted and have the potential to evolve (Williamson, 2000). Ultimately, the third level encompasses the institutions of governance, which constitute an institutional framework influencing the functionality of specific systems, such as a cluster or territorial community (Colombelli et al., 2019; Helmke & Levitsky, 2004; Williamson, 2000; Wiseman, 2023; Zukauskaite et al., 2017). Governance embodies the internal frameworks of rules, such as the degree of collaboration, the methods for harmonizing the interests of diverse stakeholders, and the strategies for establishing objectives and developmental trajectories (Colombelli et al., 2019; Williamson, 2000).

Clusters are distinguished by two key structural characteristics. They represent spatial agglomeration within a specific region, which facilitates the development of regional and sectoral specialization (Bellandi, 2002; Bohatkiewicz & Gancarczyk, 2018; Bohatkiewicz-Czaicka & Gancarczyk, 2024; Krugman, 1991; Porter, 1998). Furthermore, these structures feature network connections between enterprises and non-profit organizations, as well as universities and representatives of local government units, who foster the development and dissemination of innovations (Asheim & Isaksen, 2003; Bohatkiewicz-Czaicka & Gancarczyk, 2024; Gancarczyk & Gancarczyk, 2013; Gancarczyk, 2013; Markusen, 1996; Porter, 2000).

Clusters, unlike corporations or networks, are dynamic ecosystems where efficiency and innovation arise from local cooperation and competition. They are embedded in a regulatory, cultural, and economic framework that significantly influences their development and role in global value chains (Bohatkiewicz-Czaicka & Gancarczyk, 2025; De Gioannis et al., 2024). Clusters emerge as cohesive frameworks that foster collaboration, innovation, and resilience through structured interdependencies and shared strategic goals.

Institutional theory constitutes an approach that emphasizes the influence of formal and informal rules, norms, and shared practices in shaping the context and ecosystem within which clusters operate, with particular emphasis on the formation, stability, and adaptability of clusters (Asheim et al., 2019).

Institutional theory emphasizes regional elements such as supportive policies, entrepreneurial cultural norms, and social networks that foster clustering (Porter, 1998).

Institutional theory highlights the importance of regulatory, governance, and standard frameworks for cluster stability, cohesion, and preventing fragmentation (Asheim et al., 2006; Porter, 1998; Scott, 2008). Institutional embeddedness aligns cluster enterprises with regional and national goals, supporting sustainable initiatives. Intermediary institutions, such as trade associations and innovation hubs, enhance stability by facilitating interactions and resolving disputes (Asheim et al., 2006; Porter, 1998; Scott, 2008).

Embeddedness positively affects clusters by fostering collaboration and reducing costs through shared norms and trust. However, too much embeddedness can cause institutional lock-in, hindering innovation and adaptability (Yongsheng et al., 2021). Therefore, maintaining a balance between this local embeddedness and openness to global influences becomes essential for clusters to maintain their long-term competitiveness (Kitsos et al., 2023; Zhao et al., 2023).

The Governance as Institutional Characteristics of Clusters

The institutional nature of clusters is linked to coordination mechanisms, especially within global value chains. These governance structures regulate economic systems, influencing their efficiency and transformation (Colombelli et al., 2019; Colombo et al., 2019; Gancarczyk & Konopa, 2021; Markusen, 1996; Williamson, 2005). Cluster governance is a complex theoretical construct consisting of interconnected variables that shape management and coordination in clusters. It includes institutions of governance that form the framework that influence the operation and sustainability of clusters or territorial communities (Colombelli et al., 2019; Helmke & Levitsky, 2004; Williamson, 2000; Zukauskaite et al., 2017).

Forms of governance regulate economic exchanges and encompass market, firm, and hybrids (Williamson, 1985). Gancarczyk and Konopa (2021) conceptualize these forms as institutional structures or rules governing economic systems, clusters, and ecosystems (Colombelli et al., 2019; Helmke & Levitsky, 2004; Williamson, 2000, 2005; Zukauskaite et al., 2017). According to Gereffi (1994), a coordination structure is characterized by power relationships that regulate resource deployment along the value chain. Coordination forms establish a comprehensive framework of economic, legal, and social rules, thus influencing efficiency and change (Gancarczyk & Konopa, 2021; Markusen, 1996; Williamson, 2005). They impact clusters' relationships and embeddedness with global chains, potentially catalyzing structural change. Coordination in global chains elucidates who orchestrates the value chain and by what means, without necessarily conferring property rights (Gereffi et al., 2005).

Cluster governance includes internal rules covering participation density, leadership typologies, collaboration, partnerships, entrepreneurial activities, and public funding (Brown & Mason, 2017; Colombelli et al., 2019; Williamson, 2000). Governance allows the analysis of industrial structures and new energy technologies (Gereffi & Fernandez-Stark, 2016). It provides rules and mechanisms for collaboration and environmental interaction, determining decision making, resource allocation, knowledge transfer, innovation, and adaptability.

Institutions of governance are instrumental in directing activities and interactions within clusters to ensure conformity with overarching economic and social objectives. By instituting coherent frameworks and strategic direction, these entities promote alignment between the dynamics of clusters and the broader goals of regional or national development. Institutional structures such as governance are conducive to drafting and implementing place-based policies.

The governance depends on factors such as: i) complexity of transactions and information, particularly regarding the product and the processes surrounding its creation, ii) level of codification of information and knowledge related to the industry's technology, and iii) capabilities (resources and skills) of suppliers (Gereffi et al., 2005). Value chain types are determined by transaction complexity, codification capacity, and supplier capabilities. High complexity with low codification and limited supplier ability can stop relationship efforts like outsourcing. Relational coordination features low codification and high supplier capability (Ashenbaum, 2018). These elements define five structures: market, hierarchy, and three networks—modular, relational, and captive (Gereffi et al., 2005; Sturgeon et al., 2008). Captive coordination is hierarchical while relational and modular are non-hierarchical. Network relationships depend on lead firms' authority over suppliers. Lead firms manage production, allocating network roles. Coordination form factors include product complexity, asset specificity, production standardization, subcontractor and supplier competence, codifiability of transactions, transaction complexity, and stakeholder accessibility. Therefore, it is pertinent to acknowledge that clusters represent hybrid forms that integrate the cooperative dynamics intrinsic to enterprises with the competitive dynamics inherent within market structures (Porter, 1990, 1998). The institutional attributes of clusters are evident, as clusters are occasionally identified as a distinct form of coordination (Jacobs & De Man, 1996; Muizer & Hospers, 2000).

Governance, functioning as a regulatory mechanism for business exchanges, constitutes a principal framework for explaining additional benefits of clusters, such as economizing on transaction costs (Storper, 1995). The governance framework within industrial agglomerations is characterized by institutional density and thickness, which fosters distinctive, untraded interdependencies among regional actors (Storper, 1995). Consequently, network governance, which represents a hybrid approach to coordinating economic activities between the market and the firm, is recognized as a fundamental characteristic of clusters, in addition to industrial concentration (Markusen, 1996; Saxenian, 2000).

The network-based characteristics of clusters underscore the significance of the composition of stakeholders and the nature of relationships between them, in conjunction with the institutions that furnish the operational framework and constitute the foundation of their effectiveness (Bohatkiewicz & Gancarczyk, 2018; Bohatkiewicz-Czaicka & Gancarczyk, 2025; Williamson, 2000). The interactions among the members of the cluster manifest as vertical and horizontal linkages, as well as institutional connections (Jacobs & De Man, 1996; Muizer & Hospers, 2000), frequently employing shared technologies, accompanied by the presence of a central actor. The efficacy of a cluster is contingent on the quality of collaboration among the constituent entities (Bohatkiewicz & Gancarczyk, 2018; Jacobs & De Man, 1996; Lis & Lis, 2021, 2023).

Cluster coordination mechanisms are fundamentally institutional, with both formal and informal network linkages dependent on shared resources, including products, services, and human capital (Porter, 2000; Rosenfeld, 2002). Contemporary clusters operate internationally to lower costs and access global resources. Their competitiveness is based on network cooperation rather than geographical concentration. Proximity aids knowledge sharing and cost reduction but requires many specialized entities for greater benefits. Smaller networks have limited impact, affecting only specific areas (Bohatkiewicz-Czaicka & Gancarczyk, 2024, 2025; Jankowska, 2012).

Institutional Dynamics of Clusters as Cooperative Network Structures

The theories of network are a grounding for the cluster as institutional structures' approach (Menzel & Fornahl, 2010; Tushman & Rosenkopf, 1992). Within this framework, the degree of technological heterogeneity between firms along with the degree of network openness and flexibility delineate the emergence, development, maintenance, decline, or renewal of industrial agglomerations (Neffke et al., 2011; Ter Wal & Boschma, 2011). The concept of cluster evolution accentuates the significance of firm capabilities and networks, which serve to facilitate knowledge spillovers within the cluster and its external, international milieu (Ter Wal & Boschma, 2011). Approaches to the life cycle and evolution of clusters emphasize the critical role of endogenous factors, such as governance, alongside the firms' technological and capability endowments, for the dynamics of industrial agglomerations (Fornahl et al., 2015; Gancarczyk, 2015).

The definitions and structural characteristics of clusters underscore that they derive competitive advantage from network cooperation and geographical proximity, not just spatial concentration, fostering knowledge diffusion, economies of scale, and reduced transaction costs, especially with a critical mass of specialized entities. Notably, cooperation among a limited number of entities yields restricted impacts, confined to specific networks rather than extending to broader territorial advantages. Network collaboration facilitates enterprises' growth and the development of clusters within particular industries. This conceptual framework has significantly influenced public policies that support cluster organizations, cluster initiatives, regional innovation networks, and regional innovation systems. Although these entities share similarities with clusters, they exhibit unique characteristics (Lis & Lis, 2021, 2023). Although clusters are comparable to these industrial organizational forms, each possesses its own distinct institutional attributes.

The institutional framework of clusters is manifested through cluster initiatives and cluster organizations, which formalize and structure cooperative efforts among a variety of stakeholders (Bohatkiewicz-Czaicka & Gancarczyk, 2025). A cluster initiative refers to a formalized agreement among cluster members—encompassing businesses, public administration, and universities—to regulate collaboration, formulate strategies, and facilitate negotiations for growth and innovation (Dzierżanowski, 2012; Palmen & Baron, 2016). These initiatives are crucial in promoting education and the dissemination of advanced technical knowledge and innovations within closely situated industries (Sölvell et al., 2003).

The coordination of such initiatives may occur with or without a designated entity, referred to as a cluster organization (Szultka, 2012). A cluster organization functions as a public-private institutional entity, often endowed with legal personality, representing the cluster initiative in activities such as obtaining external funding, executing projects, and formalizing agreements (Kładź-Postolska, 2019). These organizations primarily engage in "soft" activities, such as fostering collaboration, facilitating knowledge exchange, and enhancing communication, while also participating in complex ventures such as capital partnerships to finance and undertake commercial projects (Szultka, 2012). Although clusters frequently emerge spontaneously, characterized by critical mass and specialization, cluster initiatives and organizations function as formalized frameworks that support these naturally occurring structures. They serve as institutional mechanisms that encourage the development of emerging clusters or strengthen less advanced agglomerations, establishing the foundation for long-term growth and regional specialization.

Clusters are key to regional innovation systems and networks, highlighting their role as economic entities. Similarly, regional innovation networks emphasize formal cooperation among regional firms to boost innovation (European Commission, 2002). This partnership relies on trust and shared rules to support firms' innovations. Unlike clusters, which focus on spatial or industrial concentration, innovation networks connect diverse industries to foster innovation. Clusters often involve informal collaboration, whereas innovation networks require formal agreements (Bohatkiewicz-Czaicka & Gancarczyk, 2025).

Regional innovation systems offer an expansive institutional framework, integrating not only enterprises, but also entities from the broader business milieu, including institutions for the dissemination of knowledge, financial support, and technical counsel (Cooke, 1998; European Commission, 2002). The majority of clusters operate within regional innovation systems due to their emphasis on knowledge dissemination and innovation stimulation. Nevertheless, not all regional innovation systems are classified as clusters, as they are not inherently characterized by the concentration of companies or industry specialization (Asheim & Isaksen, 2002).

1.3 The Role of Clusters and Institutions in Industrial Transitions

The Significance of Clusters in Industrial Transitions

Industrial clusters together with entrepreneurial ecosystems (EEs) and institutions are capable of creating collaborative environments which facilitate the achievement of industrial transformation (European Commission, 2020; Gancarczyk, 2019; Gancarczyk & Ujwary-Gil, 2020; Götz, 2020, 2021; Mason & Brown, 2014; Stam, 2015).

The institutional paradigm concerning industrial transitions emphasizes the coevolutionary dynamics between industry, clusters, and institutions, comprehended as encompassing rules, regulations, and associated actors (Benner, 2022; Gong & Hassink, 2019). A successful industrial transition relies on robust collaboration among a diverse set of stakeholders including clusters. These relationships enable productive dialogue, build consensus, and balance conflicting interests and priorities. Actively involving stakeholders throughout all phases of the policymaking process fosters inclusivity, improves the legitimacy of policies, and ensures that no key interest groups are excluded (OECD, 2023). This participatory approach is critical to achieving a just transition that aligns with societal expectations and gains wider acceptance among citizens, especially in markets with past experiences of difficult systemic transformations. This stakeholder-inclusive model leads to inclusive growth in industrial transition (OECD, 2023).

The industry's progression towards industrial transformation, and more specifically towards its advanced form, sustainable industrial transformation must be analyzed from the perspective of the role of cluster governance in either facilitating or obstructing the transformation. Therefore, it is essential to identify the characteristics of cluster governance that favor or impede these transition processes (Bohatkiewicz-Czaicka & Gancarczyk, 2025; Micek et al., 2021; Surwillo, 2022). Knowledge about the nature of cluster governance in practice is also valuable in the process of forming and developing cluster-based policies.

Institutional Paradigm Concerning Industrial Transitions

The coevolutionary perspective leading to sustainable industrial transformation comes from the belief that industrial policy should be a strategy to promote "high-road competitiveness," understood as the ability of an economy to achieve "beyond-GDP" goals (Aiginger, 2015). The NIP is a comprehensive framework designed to impact the entire economy, targeting macroeconomic challenges such as competitive pressures from emerging markets, the impact of the financial crisis, and observation of how reduced manufacturing activity combined with current account deficits delayed economic recovery (Aiginger, 2015). NIP focuses on new technologies and aims to align with other policies to support long-term social and environmental goals. Aiginger (2015) suggests four changes for European growth and industrial policy: i) shift from GDP to "beyond-GDP" goals, ii) redefine competitiveness as achieving broader societal goals, iii) differentiate between "low-road" and "high-road" competitiveness strategies, and iv) use industrial policy to promote high-road competitiveness. NIP should act as an intermediary between industrial and energy policies, promoting emission reductions and increasing the use of renewable energy. Implementing this policy framework requires overcoming resistance and political challenges hindering sustainable industrial ambitions (Aiginger, 2015). NIP should recognize policy-industry interactions in a localized, tailored approach involving regional and local governments to develop necessary laws and regulations (Gancarczyk & Ujwary-Gil, 2020; Grillitsch, 2015; Kitson, 2019). Stakeholders in regional or local NIP development include clusters, knowledge and technology transfer entities like technology parks and research centers, enterprise support, and non-corporate actors (Asheim et al., 2019; Gancarczyk & Ujwary-Gil, 2020; Gancarczyk et al., 2023; Hassink et al., 2019).

The institutional and coevolutionary perspectives on industrial organization highlight the dynamic interactions between industry and innovation policies. The trajectory of change and the interplay between policies and industry are characterized by a bilateral and feedback-driven dynamic.

First, the influence of policy (which is a direct manifestation of the influence of institutions) on industry tends to be deliberate and centralized (Gancarczyk et al., 2023). Within this framework, policies can assume distinct functions: they may oppose industrial change (contradicting transformation), reinforce it (leading and amplifying transformation), accommodate it (adapting to ongoing transformation), complement it (providing supplemental support), or substitute for it (proactively driving transformation) (Fothergill et al., 2019; Gancarczyk et al., 2023; Helmke & Levitsky, 2004; Hooton & Tyler, 2019; Zukauskaite et al., 2017).

On the other hand, the influence exerted by industry on policy is characteristically more decentralized, mediated through interest groups, and contingent upon the inclusiveness of policymaking frameworks, as well as the organizational capacities of enterprises (Foray et al., 2012; Fothergill et al., 2019; Hooton & Tyler, 2019).

The roles assumed by policy or industry possess the capacity to markedly influence the trajectory of structural change, serving either as facilitators or impediments in the attainment of regional industrial transformation or subsequently SIT (Frenken & Boschma, 2007). These roles have the potential to drive transformative processes by promoting alignment and synergy between industrial innovation and policy imperatives (Foray, 2014), or alternatively, they can hinder progress through the creation of misalignments, resistance, or unintended outcomes (Grillitsch, 2015; Grillitsch & Asheim, 2018; Martin & Sunley, 2006). Their impact is dependent upon the degree to which they support or obstruct the requisite adjustments in industrial structures and governance frameworks necessary for sustainable and inclusive transformation (Hassink, 2010; Zukauskaite et al., 2017).

However, it is imperative to emphasize that the policies directed specifically toward energy clusters are presently in the initial phases of development concerning ecosystemic governance structures and industrial transitions (Dragan, 2020; Elzen & Wieczorek, 2005; Grigore & Dragan, 2020; Mirowski & Kubica, 2016). The existing body of literature and research on the interrelations between energy clusters and policy is primarily based on qualitative case studies (Afeltowicz et al., 2024; Micek et al., 2021; Surwillo, 2022). Consequently, a comprehensive examination of specific phenomena related to cluster-based policies, particularly through the example of energy clusters as a phenomenon leading to ESIT, is of significant value, underdeveloped in literature, and research achievements, i.e., in the scope of industrial transformation, institutional economics, and industry economics.

1.4 Institutional and Evolutionary Approach to Cluster Development

Theoretical Framework for Institutional Approach to Cluster Development

Cluster evolution, alternatively termed *cluster development*, can be conceptualized as a progression through successive stages of development, consequent upon alterations in cluster structure. Consequently, structural change signifies modifications in the defining characteristics of the cluster, such as spatial and industrial agglomeration, industrial profile, and networking system (Bohatkiewicz & Gancarczyk, 2018; Gancarczyk, 2013).

The theory of clusters has undergone significant development with a focus on dynamic approaches, including path dependencies (Asheim et al., 2019; Grillitsch & Asheim, 2018; Hassink et al., 2019; Isaksen et al., 2019), cluster evolution, life cycles (Fornahl et al., 2015), and clusters' position changes in global value chains (upgrading and downgrading) (Bohatkiewicz, 2018; Bohatkiewicz-Czaicka & Gancarczyk, 2024, 2025; De Marchi et al., 2017; Gancarczyk & Bohatkiewicz, 2018; Humphrey & Schmitz, 2000, 2002). Although there is a significant literature concerning institutional approach, types of path development, regional industrial transformation, and industrial transformation itself, yet there remains a significant research gap concerning the cooccurrence and interdependence between institutional and evolutionary approaches and cluster development (Parrilli, 2024).

In the volatile context of clusters, the institutional environment plays a key role in their evolution. Institutional theory highlights the adaptability in clusters as crucial for responding to economic and technological changes. Clusters with flexible institutional frameworks, such as adaptive governance, evolving norms, and responsive education systems, are better prepared to adopt new technologies, enter new markets, or restructure during crises (Frenken et al., 2015). Adaptability helps clusters deal with technological lock-ins and economic disruptions, maintaining their relevance and competitiveness globally. Institutional theory offers insight into the roles of institutions in shaping the cluster's life cycle and resilience.

Clusters are deeply rooted in regional and national institutions, influencing their formation and growth. Regional institutions, such as local governments and educational bodies, support clusters with specific policies, funding, and infrastructure. The proximity to universities and research centers promotes knowledge spillovers and sharing, while regional policies promote collaboration within clusters.

Development Paths as an Element of the Cluster Development Process

The evolution of territorial industrial structures can be described through development paths. The phenomena of globalization and digitization have introduced challenges to the internal structures of clusters, increasing their vulnerability to international competition and collaboration, thus intensifying the issue of cluster transformation. Industrial transformations such as regional industrial transformation and sustainable industrial transformations lead to changes and shifts in the industrial structure, namely path trajectories (Asheim, 2019; Grillitsch & Asheim, 2018; Isaksen et al., 2019). Industrial path trajectories include advancements within established industries, the emergence and expansion of new industries within a region, and the decline and eventual disappearance of existing industries (Asheim et al., 2019; Foray, 2014; Grillitsch et al., 2018). Developments in existing industries include path extension and path renewal. The first is understood as an enhancement of established industries through incremental innovations within existing technological pathways. The latter means significant transformations in existing industries as they move up value chains, driven by improvements in skills and production capabilities, or by the adoption of new technologies, organizational innovations, or business models. The formation and development of new industries within a region can manifest also as a path branching, which involves related diversification, or path creation, which involves unrelated diversification.

Path branching denotes the formation of new industries that originate from the competencies and knowledge inherent in preexisting regional industries. These emerging industries are contiguous to established ones in terms of technologies, products, and markets. Path creation denotes the development and expansion of novel industries that bear no connection to preexisting regional industries. The process in which established industries experience decline and eventual dissolution can be described as path exhaustion. This phenomenon occurs when emerging industries provide alternatives to technologically and socially outdated solutions or when incumbent industries experience stagnation or regression (Asheim et al., 2019; Grillitsch et al., 2018; Hassink et al., 2019; Isaksen et al., 2019).

Moreover, the dynamics of individual industries, highlighted by path trajectories, are not the only one sphere that the institutional approach influences. Regional industrial transformation and sustainable industrial transformation are broader phenomena that also lead to cluster development processes (Hassink et al., 2019; Martin & Sunley, 2006). The development of a cluster is significantly influenced by policies that are conceived and executed at multiple levels, such as cluster-based policies and industrial policies, which bear a diverse range of impacts: local, regional, national, or international.

The Stages and Determinants of Cluster Development

The evolutionary approach to cluster development is also based on the development stages of clusters and entrepreneurial ecosystems as related phenomena. The cluster's development includes four stages, namely: i) inception or growth through exploration and exploitation of knowledge, ii) maturity through exploitation of knowledge with limited exploration, iii) threat of decline through rigid specialization and lock-in, and iv) renewal through renewed exploration and exploitation of knowledge (Gancarczyk, 2013). The institutional approach to cluster development assumes that the development stage of a cluster can be assessed based on variables such as the density of cluster participants (in different categories), intensity of entrepreneurial activity, collaboration and international linkages, and public financing (Gancarczyk & Konopa, 2021).

Entrepreneurial ecosystems can serve as reflections of industrial clusters, representing business and economic phenomena. Consequently, the evolutionary trajectory pursued by EEs could also be applied to clusters, given their intrinsic connection to EEs, characterized by mutual coupling and interaction (cluster-EE and EE-cluster). Therefore, the developmental phases of entrepreneurial ecosystems be correlated with the developmental milestones of the clusters themselves.

Colombelli, Paolucci, and Ughetto (2019) provide a conceptual framework for understanding entrepreneurial ecosystem evolution, emphasizing the role of institutional structures in fostering collaboration. Their model highlights three key stages: the birth phase, characterized by limited internal collaboration; the transition phase, reflecting intermediate levels of collaboration; and the consolidation phase, where collaboration becomes robust and well structured. This progression underscores the institutional mechanisms that guide the development and strengthening of entrepreneurial networks.

Similarly, Brown and Mason (2017) delineate embryonic (early stage) and scale-up (developed) entrepreneurial ecosystems based on attributes such as the intensity of entrepreneurial activities, high-growth enterprises (HGEs), collaboration networks, international linkages, and public funding. They stress that the institutional environment, from governance to public investment, plays a pivotal role in enabling the transition from embryonic stages to mature, developed ecosystems.

Given that many entrepreneurial ecosystems remain in the transition stage, a three-stage framework effectively captures their evolution in relation to institutional governance. This framework spans the phases of birth, transition, and consolidation, marked by increasing entrepreneurial activity, enhanced international connections, and deeper socio-business collaboration. It also reflects a shift in governance from reliance on public support in early stages to a more autonomous and integrated ecosystem at maturity, driven by institutional coordination and support. Governance structures are important in shaping the performance and dynamics of territorial units, such as clusters or entrepreneurial ecosystems (Cho et al., 2021; Mack & Mayer, 2016).

As an organizational and coordination structure within the industrial sector, which is intricately linked to the institutional sphere, a cluster of is an element of a larger socioeconomic system on a given territory (Ottati, 2002). It is distinguished by intersectoral horizontal and vertical linkages that are regulated not only by policy frameworks but also by a leading entity (also referred to as a leading firm or lead firm) while being embedded in networks such as global value chains (Jacobs & De Man, 1996; Muizer & Hospers, 2000; OECD, 2005). Clusters demonstrate considerable variability in their level of integration within the expansive network of enterprises and entities that constitute the business environment (Trippl et al., 2015). This differentiation pertains to the clusters' developmental status, encompassing their evolutionary trajectory or specific phase within the life cycle, as articulated by Martin and Sunley (2007) and further elaborated by Bergman (2008). Furthermore, the heterogeneity of the clusters can be attributed to factors such as the degree of spatial concentration of industries, the extent of regional specialization, and the organizational structures and characteristics of the relationships existing among members of the industrial agglomeration. These variations collectively highlight the complex nature of clusters and their dependence on contextual and structural factors.

On a national scale, comprehensive institutional structures, including regulatory frameworks, fiscal policies, and national innovation strategies, determine the development stages and consequently the competitive edge of clusters. Advantageous tax policies or industry-specific regulations can establish a conducive milieu for clusters to flourish. Moreover, national institutions frequently facilitate the incorporation of clusters into global value chains, affecting their access to international markets and technologies.

Diverse governance frameworks, in relation to foundational principles, collaborative interactions between social and business entities, channels of knowledge, and stages of development, can exert varying influences on outcomes such as productive high-growth entrepreneurship, which is also linked to cluster activities and their effectiveness. Clusters, particularly those occupying prominent positions within global value chains, frequently incorporate such HGEs. Entities that are highly active and effective are also likely to achieve superior performance as integral components of broader organizational structures within the economy. This is notably significant from the perspective of a cluster's competitiveness, as well as its potential to advance, renew, or avert decline.

References

Afeltowicz, Ł., Nawojczyk, M., & Tyrała, R. (2024). Entrepreneurial actions in energy transition: A study of three local energy clusters in Poland. *European Urban and Regional Studies*, *31*(2), 132–148. https://doi.org/10.1177/09697764231179667

Aiginger, K. (2015). Industrial policy for a sustainable growth path. In D. Bailey, K. Cowling, & P. Tomlinson (Eds.), *New perspectives on industrial policy for a modern Britain* (pp. 364–394). Oxford University Press. https://doi.org/10.1093/acprof:oso/9780198706205.003.0019

Aiginger, K., & Rodrik, D. (2020). Rebirth of industrial policy and an agenda for the twenty-first century. *Journal of Industry, Competition and Trade*, *20*(2), 189–207. https://doi.org/10.1007/s10842-019-00322-3

Andreoni, A., Frattini, F., & Prodi, G. (2024). Getting robots in 'our own hands': Structural drivers, spatial dynamics and multi-scalar industrial policy in China. *Competition & Change*. https://doi.org/10.1177/10245294241261878

Asheim, B. T. (2019). Smart specialisation, innovation policy and regional innovation systems: What about new path development in less innovative regions? *Innovation: The European Journal of Social Science Research*, *32*(1), 8–25. https://doi.org/10.1080/13511610.2018.1491001

Asheim, B. T., Cooke, P., & Martin, R. (2006). *Clusters and regional development: Critical reflections and explorations*. Routledge. https://www.routledge.com/Clusters-and-Regional-Development-Critical-Reflections-and-Explorations/Asheim-Cooke-Martin/p/book/9780415578622

Asheim, B. T., & Isaksen, A. (2002). Regional innovation systems: The integration of local "sticky" and global "ubiquitous" knowledge. *Journal of Technology Transfer*, *27*(1), 77–86. https://doi.org/10.1023/A:1013100704794

Asheim, B. T., & Isaksen, A. (2003). SMEs and the regional dimension of innovation. In B. T. Asheim, A. Isaksen, C. Nauwelaers, & F. Tödtling (Eds.), *Regional innovation policy for small-medium enterprises* (pp. 21–46). Edward Elgar Publishing.

Asheim, B. T., Isaksen, A., & Trippl, M. (2019). *Advanced introduction to regional innovation systems*. Edward Elgar Publishing.

Ashenbaum, B. (2018). From market to hierarchy: An empirical assessment of a supply chain governance typology. *Journal of Purchasing and Supply Management*, *24*(1), 59–67. https://doi.org/10.1016/j.pursup.2017.06.002

Ashford, N. A., Hafkamp, W., Prakke, F., & Vergragt, P. (2007). *Pathways to sustainable industrial transformations: Co-optimising competitiveness, employment, and environment*. https://dspace.mit.edu/handle/1721.1/41844

Ayrapetyan, D., & Hermans, F. (2020). Introducing a multiscalar framework for biocluster research: A meta-analysis. *Sustainability*, *12*(9), 3890. https://doi.org/10.3390/su12093890

Bailey, D., Glasmeier, A., & Tomlinson, P. R. (2019). Industrial policy back on the agenda: Putting industrial policy in its place? *Cambridge Journal of Regions, Economy and Society*, 319–326. https://doi.org/10.1093/cjres/rsz018

Bellandi, M. (2002). Italian Industrial districts: An Industrial economics interpretation. *European Planning Studies*, *10*(4), 425–437. https://doi.org/10.1080/09654310220130158

Benner, M. (2022). Retheorizing industrial–institutional coevolution: A multidimensional perspective. *Regional Studies*, *56*(9), 1524–1537. https://doi.org/10.1080/00343404.2021.1949441

Bergal, O. (2020). Innovative energy clusters' infrastructure. *International Journal of Economics & Business Administration (IJEBA)*, *VIII*(Special 1), 361–376.

Bergman, E. M. (2008). Cluster life cycles: An emerging synthesis. In C. Karlsson (Ed.), *Handbook of research in cluster theory* (pp. 114–132). Edward Elgar Publishing.

Bohatkiewicz, J. (2018). Factors facilitating upgrading process of knowledge-intensive business services' clusters in global value chains. *Przedsiębiorczość i Zarządzanie*, *19*(2.1), 19–27.

Bohatkiewicz, J., & Gancarczyk, M. (2018). *Structural characteristics of industrial clusters: The essence and measurement*. Wyższa Szkoła Biznesu-National-Louis University. https://ruj.uj.edu.pl/xmlui/handle/item/57094

Bohatkiewicz-Czaicka, J., & Gancarczyk, M. (2024). *Ewolucja koncepcji klastrów a uwarunkowania ich globalnej pozycji*. Wydawnictwo UJ.

Bohatkiewicz-Czaicka, J., & Gancarczyk, M. (2025). *Industrial clusters in international value chains: Conceptual advancement and empirical evidence from European ICT clusters*. Taylor & Francis.

Brown, R., & Mason, C. (2017). Looking inside the spiky bits: A critical review and conceptualisation of entrepreneurial ecosystems. *Small Business Economics*, *49*(1), 11–30. https://doi.org/10.1007/s11187-017-9865-7

Chen, Y., & Hassink, R. (2020). Multi-scalar knowledge bases for new regional industrial path development: Toward a typology. *European Planning Studies*, *28*(12), 2489–2507. https://doi.org/10.1080/09654313.2020.1724265

Cho, D. S., Ryan, P., & Buciuni, G. (2021). Evolutionary entrepreneurial ecosystems: A research pathway. *Small Business Economics*, *58*, 1865–1883.

Ciffolilli, A., & Muscio, A. (2018). Industry 4.0: National and regional comparative advantages in key enabling technologies. *European Planning Studies*, *26*(12), 2323–2343. https://doi.org/10.1080/09654313.2018.1529145

Coenen, L., Hansen, T., Glasmeier, A., & Hassink, R. (2021). Regional foundations of energy transitions. *Cambridge Journal of Regions, Economy and Society*, *14*(2), 219–233. https://doi.org/10.1093/cjres/rsab010

Colombelli, A., Paolucci, E., & Ughetto, E. (2019). Hierarchical and relational governance and the life cycle of entrepreneurial ecosystems. *Small Business Economics*, *52*, 505–521.

Colombo, M. G., Dagnino, G. B., Lehman, E. E., & Salmador, M. (2019). The governance of entrepreneurial ecosystems. *Small Business Economics*, *52*, 419–428.

Cooke, P. (1998). *Introduction. Origins of the concept* (H.-J. Braczyk, & M. Heidenreich, Eds.). UCL Press.

De Gioannis, E., Dudka, A., & Łapniewska, Z. (2024). Gender stereotypes and empowerment of women in energy cooperatives: A comparative analysis from Italy and Belgium. *Energy Research & Social Science*, *116*, 103673. https://doi.org/10.1016/j.erss.2024.103673

Delgado, M., Porter, M. E., & Stern, S. (2016). Defining clusters of related industries. *Journal of Economic Geography*, *16*(1), 1–38. https://doi.org/10.1093/jeg/lbv017

De Marchi, V., Gereffi, G., & Grandinetti, R. (2017). Evolutionary trajectories of industrial districts in global value chains. In V. De Marchi, G. Gereffi, & R. Grandinetti (Eds.), *Local clusters in global value chains: Linking actors and territories through manufacturing and innovation*. https://doi.org/10.4324/9781315182049

Dragan, D. (2020). Legal barriers to the development of energy clusters in Poland. *European Energy and Environmental Law Review*, *29*(1), 14–20.

Dzierżanowski, M. (red). (2012). *Kierunki i założenia polityki klastrowej w Polsce do 2020 roku Rekomendacje Grupy roboczej ds. Polityki klastrowej.*

Elzen, B., & Wieczorek, A. (2005). Transitions towards sustainability through system innovation. *Technological Forecasting and Social Change*, *72*(6), 651–661.

European Commission (2002). *Regional clusters in Europe. Observatory of European SMEs* (Vol. 2). Office for Official Publications of the European Communities.

European Commission (2020). *A New Industrial Strategy for Europe*. https://eur-lex.europa.eu/legal-content/EN/TXT/?qid=1593086905382&uri=CELEX:52020DC0102

Foray, D. (2014). *Smart specialisation*. Routledge. https://doi.org/10.4324/9781315773063

Foray, D., Goddard, J., Beldarrain, X. G., Landabaso, M., McCann, P., Morgan, K., Nauwelaers, C., & Ortega-Argilés, R. (2012). *Guide to research and innovation strategies for smart specialisations* (Europe). https://apo.org.au/node/90736

Fornahl, D., Hassink, R., & Menzel, M.-P. (2015). Broadening our knowledge on cluster evolution. *European Planning Studies*, *23*(10), 1921–1931. https://doi.org/10.1080/09654313.2015.1016654

Fothergill, S., Gore, T., & Wells, P. (2019). Industrial strategy and the UK regions: Sectorally narrow and spatially blind. *Cambridge Journal of Regions, Economy and Society*, *12*(3), 445–466. https://doi.org/10.1093/cjres/rsz016

Frenken, K., & Boschma, R. A. (2007). A theoretical framework for evolutionary economic geography: Industrial dynamics and urban growth as a branching process. *Journal of Economic Geography*, *7*(5), 635–649. https://doi.org/10.1093/jeg/lbm018

Frenken, K., Cefis, E., & Stam, E. (2015). Industrial dynamics and clusters: A survey. *Regional Studies*, *49*(1), 10–27. https://doi.org/10.1080/00343404.2014.904505

Gancarczyk, M. (2010). Model schyłku i odrodzenia klastrów. *Gospodarka Narodowa*, *3*, 1–21.

Gancarczyk, M. (2013). Externality-based model of cluster evolution. *Recenzowane Materiały Konferencyjne, Cykliczna Konferencja Naukowa Regional Innovation Policies, 10-11 Października 2013.*

Gancarczyk, M. (2015). Enterprise- and industry-level drivers of cluster evolution and their outcomes for clusters from developed and less-developed countries. *European Planning Studies, 23*(10), 1932–1952. https://doi.org/10.1080/09654313.2014.959811

Gancarczyk, M. (2019). The performance of high-growers and regional entrepreneurial ecosystems: A research framework. *Entrepreneurial Business and Economics Review, 7*(3), 99–123. https://doi.org/10.15678/EBER.2019.070306

Gancarczyk, M., & Bohatkiewicz, J. (2018). Research streams in cluster upgrading. A literature review. *Journal of Entrepreneurship, Management and Innovation, 14*(4), 17–42. https://doi.org/10.7341/20181441

Gancarczyk, M., & Konopa, S. (2021). *Exploring the governance of entrepreneurial ecosystems for productive high growth.* Foresight and STI Governance, 15(4). https://foresight-journal.hse.ru/article/view/19148

Gancarczyk, M., Najda-Janoszka, M., Gancarczyk, J., & Hassink, R. (2023). Exploring regional innovation policies and regional industrial transformation from a coevolutionary perspective: The case of Małopolska, Poland. *Economic Geography, 99*(1), 51–80. https://doi.org/10.1080/00130095.2022.2120465

Gancarczyk, M., & Ujwary-Gil, A. (2020). *Revitalizing industrial policy through smart, micro-level and bottom-up approaches.* In A. Ujwary-Gil, & M. Gancarczyk (Eds.), New challenges in economic policy, business, and management. Polska Akademia Nauk. https://konferencja.jemi.edu.pl/files/Ujwary-Gil_Gancarczyk_monografia_2020.pdf

Gancarczyk, M., & Gancarczyk, J. (2013). Structural change in industrial clusters—Scenarios and policy implications. *Studia Regionalia, 35*, 111–127.

Gereffi, G. (1994). *The Organization of Buyer-Driven Global Commodity Chains: How U.S. Retailers Shape Overseas Production Networks.* 95–122.

Gereffi, G., & Fernandez-Stark, K. (2016). Global Value Chain Analysis: A Primer. *Center on Globalization, Governance & Competitivenes (CGGC), July*, 1–39.

Gereffi, G., Humphrey, J., & Sturgeon, T. (2005). The governance of global value chains. *Review of International Political Economy, 12*(1), 78–104. https://doi.org/10.1080/09692290500049805

Gong, H., & Hassink, R. (2019). Co-evolution in contemporary economic geography: Towards a theoretical framework. *Regional Studies, 53*(9), 1344–1355. https://doi.org/10.1080/00343404.2018.1494824

Gong, H., & Hassink, R. (2020). Context sensitivity and economic-geographic (re)theorising. *Cambridge Journal of Regions, Economy and Society, 13*(3), 475–490. https://doi.org/10.1093/cjres/rsaa021

Götz, M. (2020). Cluster role in industry 4.0–a pilot study from Germany. *Competitiveness Review: An International Business Journal, 31*(1), 54–82.

Götz, M. (2021). *Clusters, digital transformation and regional development in Germany.* Routledge.

Grigore, A. M., & Dragan, I. M. (2020). Towards sustainable entrepreneurial ecosystems in a transitional economy: An analysis of two Romanian city-regions through the lens of entrepreneurs. *Sustainability (Switzerland), 12*(15), 6061. https://doi.org/10.3390/su12156061

Grillitsch, M. (2015). Institutional layers, connectedness and change: Implications for economic evolution in regions. *European Planning Studies, 23*(10), 2099–2124.

Grillitsch, M., & Asheim, B. (2018). Place-based innovation policy for industrial diversification in regions. *European Planning Studies, 26*(8), 1638–1662. https://doi.org/10.1080/09654313.2018.1484892

Grillitsch, M., Asheim, B., & Trippl, M. (2018). Unrelated knowledge combinations: The unexplored potential for regional industrial path development. *Cambridge Journal of Regions, Economy and Society, 11*(2), 257–274. https://doi.org/10.1093/cjres/rsy012

Hassink, R. (2010). Regional resilience: A promising concept to explain differences in regional economic adaptability? *Cambridge Journal of Regions, Economy and Society, 3*(1), 45–58. https://doi.org/10.1093/cjres/rsp033

Hassink, R., Isaksen, A., & Trippl, M. (2019). Towards a comprehensive understanding of new regional industrial path development. *Regional Studies, 53*(1), 1–10.

Helmke, G., & Levitsky, S. (2004). Informal institutions and comparative politics: A research agenda. *Perspectives on Politics, 2*(4), 725–740.

Hodgson, G. M. (2006). What are institutions? *Journal of Economic Issues, 40*(1), 1–25. https://doi.org/10.1080/00213624.2006.11506879

Hodgson, G. M. (2015). On defining institutions: Rules versus equilibria. *Journal of Institutional Economics, 11*(3), 497–505. https://doi.org/10.1017/S1744137415000028

Hooton, C. A., & Tyler, P. (2019). Do enterprise zones have a role to play in delivering a place-based industrial strategy? *Cambridge Journal of Regions, Economy and Society, 12*(3), 423–443. https://doi.org/10.1093/cjres/rsz015

Hu, X., & Hassink, R. (2020). Adaptation, adaptability and regional economic resilience: A conceptual framework. In G. Bristow, & A. Healy (Eds.), *Handbook on regional economic resilience* (pp. 54–68). Edward Elgar Publishing. https://doi.org/10.4337/9781785360862.00009

Humphrey, J., & Schmitz, H. (2000). Governance and upgrading: Linking industrial clusters and GVC research. *IDS Working Paper, 120*, 1–37.

Humphrey, J., & Schmitz, H. (2002). How does insertion in global value chains affect upgrading in industrial clusters? *Regional Studies, 36*(9), 1017–1027. https://doi.org/10.1080/0034340022000022198

Isaksen, A., Jakobsen, S.-E., Njøs, R., & Normann, R. (2019). Regional industrial restructuring resulting from individual and system agency. *Innovation: The European Journal of Social Science Research, 32*(1), 48–65. https://doi.org/10.1080/13511610.2018.1496322

Jacobs, D., & De Man, A.-P. (1996). Clusters, industrial policy and firm strategy. *Technology Analysis & Strategic Management, 8*(4), 425–438. https://doi.org/10.1080/09537329608522461

Jankowska, B. (2012). *Koopetycja w klastrach kreatywnych. Przyczynek do teorii regulacji w gospodarce rynkowej*. Wydawnictwo Uniwersytetu Ekonomicznego w Poznaniu.

Janssen, M. J., & Frenken, K. (2019). Cross-specialisation policy: Rationales and options for linking unrelated industries. *Cambridge Journal of Regions, Economy and Society, 12*(2), 195–212. https://doi.org/10.1093/cjres/rsz001

Jasiński, J., Kozakiewicz, M., & Sołtysik, M. (2021). Determinants of energy cooperatives' development in rural areas—Evidence from Poland. *Energies, 14*(2), 319. https://doi.org/10.3390/en14020319

Kitson, M. (2019). Innovation policy and place: A critical assessment. *Cambridge Journal of Regions, Economy and Society, 12*(2), 293–315. https://doi.org/10.1093/cjres/rsz007

Kitsos, T., Grabner, S. M., & Carrascal-Incera, A. (2023). Industrial embeddedness and regional economic resistance in Europe. *Economic Geography*, *99*(3), 227–252. https://doi.org/10.1080/00130095.2023.2174514

Kładź-Postolska, K. (2019). Cluster policy and business innovation. *Gospodarka Narodowa*, *297*(1), 69–86. https://doi.org/10.33119/GN/105515

Krugman, P. (1991). *Geography and trade*. MIT Press.

Lis, A. M., & Lis, A. (2021). *The cluster organization: Analyzing the development of cooperative relationships*. Routledge.

Lis, A. M., & Lis, A. (2023). *Proximity and the cluster organization*. Routledge.

Lis, A. M., McPhillips, M., & Lis, A. (2020). Sustainability of cluster organizations as open innovation intermediaries. *Sustainability*, *12*(24), 10520. https://doi.org/10.3390/su122410520

Lubacha, J., & Wendler, T. (2021). Do European firms obey the rules? Environmental innovativeness in light of institutional frameworks. *Industry and Innovation*, *28*(9), 1196–1223. https://doi.org/10.1080/13662716.2021.1929869

Luken, R., & Castellanos-Silveria, F. (2011). Industrial transformation and sustainable development in developing countries. *Sustainable Development*, *19*(3), 167–175.

Lundvall, B.-Å (1992). *National systems of innovation: Toward a theory of innovation and interactive learning*. Anthem Press.

Mack, E., & Mayer, H. (2016). The evolutionary dynamics of entrepreneurial ecosystems. *Urban Studies*, *53*(10), 2118–2133.

Manowska, A., Osadnik, K. T., & Wyganowska, M. (2017). Economic and social aspects of restructuring Polish coal mining: Focusing on Poland and the EU. *Resources Policy*, *52*, 192–200. https://doi.org/10.1016/j.resourpol.2017.02.006

Marhold, A.-A. (2015). Fragmentation and the nexus between the WTO and the ECT in global energy governance – A legal-institutional analysis twenty years later. *Journal of World Investment and Trade*, *16*(3), 389–435. https://doi.org/10.1163/22119000-01603001

Markusen, A. (1996). Sticky places in slippery space: A typology of industrial districts. *Economic Geography*, *72*(3), 293–313.

Martin, R., & Sunley, P. (2006). Path dependence and regional economic evolution. *Journal of Economic Geography*, *6*(4), 395–437. https://doi.org/10.1093/jeg/lbl012

Martin, R., & Sunley, P. (2007). Complexity thinking and evolutionary economic geography. *Journal of Economic Geography*, *7*(5), 573–601. https://doi.org/10.1093/jeg/lbm019

Mason, C., & Brown, R. (2014). Entrepreneurial ecosystems and growth oriented entrepreneurship. *Final Report to OECD*, Paris, *30*(1), Article 1.

McCauley, S. M., & Stephens, J. C. (2012). Green energy clusters and socio-technical transitions: Analysis of a sustainable energy cluster for regional economic development in Central Massachusetts, USA. *Sustainability Science*, *7*(2), 213–225. https://doi.org/10.1007/s11625-012-0164-6

Menzel, M.-P., & Fornahl, D. (2010). Cluster life cycles—Dimensions and rationales of cluster evolution. *Industrial and Corporate Change*, *19*(1), 205–238. https://doi.org/10.1093/icc/dtp036

Micek, D., Kocór, M., Worek, B., & Szczucka, A. (2021). *Społeczne uwarunkowania funkcjonowania klastrów energii w Polsce: Raport podsumowujący analizę studium przypadku wybranych klastrów: Cz. 3*. Ministerstwo Rozwoju, Pracy i Technologii, Akademia Górniczo-Hutnicza im. Stanisława Staszica w Krakowie, Narodowe

Centrum Badań Jądrowych. https://www.er.agh.edu.pl/media/filer_public/66/cb/66cb3fd2-854d-47c5-baaa-c2952fb8e639/raport_spoleczne_uwarunkowania_funkcjonowania_klastrow_energii_w_polsce.pdf

Mirowski, T., & Kubica, K. (2016). The role of biomass in energy clusters. *Polityka Energetyczna*, *19*(4), 125–138.

Mucha-Kuś, K., Sołtysik, M., Zamasz, K., & Szczepańska-Woszczyna, K. (2021). Coopetitive nature of energy communities—The energy transition context. *Energies*, *14*(4), 931. https://doi.org/10.3390/en14040931

Muizer, A., & Hospers, G.-J. (2000). *SMEs in regional industry clusters: The impact of ICT and the knowledge economy* (Issue March). Small Business Research and Conultancy.

Neffke, F., Henning, M., & Boschma, R. (2011). How do regions diversify over time? Industry relatedness and the development of new growth paths in regions. *Economic Geography*, *87*(3), 237–265. https://doi.org/10.1111/j.1944-8287.2011.01121.x

Nelson, R. R. (1993). *National innovation systems: A comparative analysis*. Oxford University Press.

North, D. C. (1990). A transaction cost theory of politics. *Journal of Theoretical Politics*, *2*(4), 355–367. https://doi.org/10.1177/0951692890002004001

North, D. C. (2008). Institutions and the performance of economies over time. In C. Ménard, & M. M. Shirley (Eds.), *Handbook of new institutional economics* (pp. 21–30). Springer. https://doi.org/10.1007/978-3-540-69305-5_2

North, D. C. (2010). *Understanding the process of economic change*. Princeton university press.

OECD (2005). *Business Clusters: Promoting Enterprise in Central and Eastern Europe*. OECD. https://doi.org/10.1787/9789264007116-en

OECD (2023). *Regions in Industrial Transition 2023: New Approaches to Persistent Problems*. OECD. https://doi.org/10.1787/5604c2ab-en

Oinas, P., Trippl, M., & Höyssä, M. (2018). Regional industrial transformations in the interconnected global economy. *Cambridge Journal of Regions, Economy and Society*, *11*(2), 227–240.

Ostrom, E. (2010). Beyond markets and states: Polycentric governance of complex economic systems. *American Economic Review*, *100*(3), 641–672.

Ottati, G. D. (2002). Social concertation and local development: The case of industrial districts. *European Planning Studies*, *10*(4), 449–466. https://doi.org/10.1080/09654310220130176

Palmen, L., & Baron, M. (2016). Przewodnik dla animatorów inicjatyw klastrowych w Polsce *(Wydanie 3., zaktualizowane)*. Polska Agencja Rozwoju Przedsiębiorczości.

Parrilli, M. D. (2024). Cluster policy: The challenging and complex horizon in the 2020s. *European Planning Studies*, *32*(9), 1868–1884. https://doi.org/10.1080/09654313.2023.2239281

Porter, M. E. (1990). *Competitive advantage of nations: Creating and sustaining superior performance*. First Free Press.

Porter, M. E. (1998). Clusters and the new economics of competition. *Harvard Business Review*, *76*(6), 77–90.

Porter, M. E. (2000). Location, competition, and economic development: Local clusters in a global economy. *Economic Development Quarterly*, *14*(1), 15–34. https://doi.org/10.1177/089124240001400105

Rosenfeld, S. A. (2002). *A Governor's Guide to Cluster-Based Economic Development* (Issue January 2002).

Saxenian, A. (2000). Regional networks in Silicon Valley and route 128. In *Regional innovation, knowledge, and global change* (pp. 123–138). Pinter.

Scott, W. R. (2008). *Institutions and organizations: Ideas and interests*. SAGE.

Sjøtun, S. G., & Njøs, R. (2019). Green reorientation of clusters and the role of policy: 'The normative' and 'the neutral' route. *European Planning Studies*, *27*(12), 2411–2430. https://doi.org/10.1080/09654313.2019.1630370

Smith, A., Stirling, A., & Berkhout, F. (2004). *Governing sustainable industrial transformation under different transition contexts*. 113–132.

Sölvell, Ö., Lindqvist, G., & Ketels, C. H. M.. (2003). The cluster initiative greenbook (1st ed.). Ivory Tower.

Stam, E. (2015). Entrepreneurial ecosystems and regional policy: A sympathetic critique. *European Planning Studies*, *23*(9), 1759–1769.

Storper, M. (1995). The resurgence of regional economies, ten years later: The region as a nexus of untraded interdependencies. *European Urban and Regional Studies*, *2*(3), 191–221. https://doi.org/10.1177/096977649500200301

Sturgeon, T., Van Biesebroeck, J., & Gereffi, G. (2008). Value chains, networks and clusters: Reframing the global automotive industry. *Journal of Economic Geography*, *8*(3), 297–321. https://doi.org/10.1093/jeg/lbn007

Surwillo, I. (2022). Energy clusters in Poland: Towards diffused green energy communities. In F. Karimi, & M. Rodi (Eds.), *Energy transition in the Baltic Sea region* (pp. 185–204). Routledge.

Sycz, P., & Wojnicka-Sycz, E. (2023). Significance of digital innovations of Industry 4.0. for Polish enterprises on the example of Podkarpackie and Lubuskie voivodeships. *Zeszyty Naukowe Politechniki Śląskiej. Organizacja i Zarządzanie*, *182*, 297–321. https://repozytorium.bg.ug.edu.pl/info/article/UOG37cb8c16021943e2b2ac89e3743172a5/. Accessed January 10, 2025.

Szultka, S. (Ed.). (2012). *Klastry w Polsce—Raport z cyklu paneli dyskusyjnych*. Polska Agencja Rozwoju Przedsiębiorczości.

Ter Wal, A. L. J., & Boschma, R. (2011). Co-evolution of firms, industries and networks in space. *Regional Studies*, *45*(7), 919–933. https://doi.org/10.1080/00343400802662658

Trejo-Nieto, A. (2021). Green industrial policies for sustainability and resilience. In R. Brears (Ed.), *The Palgrave encyclopedia of sustainable resources and ecosystem resilience* (pp. 1–18). Springer International Publishing. https://doi.org/10.1007/978-3-030-67776-3_33-1

Trippl, M., Grillitsch, M., Isaksen, A., & Sinozic, T. (2015). Perspectives on cluster evolution: Critical review and future research issues. *European Planning Studies*, *23*(10), 2028–2044. https://doi.org/10.1080/09654313.2014.999450

Tushman, M. L., & Rosenkopf, L. (1992). Organizational determinants of technological change: Toward a sociology of technological evolution. In L. L. Cummings, & B. M. Staw (Eds.), *Research in organizational behavior* (14th ed., pp. 311–347). JAI Press. https://faculty.wharton.upenn.edu/wp-content/uploads/2012/05/artitushman_rosenkopf_rob_1992.pdf

Veblen, T. (1919). *The place of science in modern civilisation*. B. W. HUEBSCH. https://www.gutenberg.org/files/39949/39949-h/39949-h.htm

Williamson, O. E. (1985). *The economic institutions of capitalism. Firms, markets, relational contracting*. The Free Press.

Williamson, O. E. (2000). The new institutional economics: Taking stock, looking ahead. *Journal of Economic Literature*, *38*(3), 595–613.

Williamson, O. E. (2005). The economics of governance. *American Economic Review*, *95*(2), 1–18. https://doi.org/10.1257/000282805774669880

Wiseman, H. J. (2023). Energy governance models. In G. Bellantuono, L. Godden, H. Mostert, H. Wiseman, & H. Zhang (Eds.), *Handbook of energy law in the low-carbon transition* (pp. 41–64). De Gruyter. https://doi.org/10.1515/9783110752403-010

Wojnicka-Sycz, E., Piróg, K., Tutaj, J., Walentynowicz, P., Sycz, P., & TenBrink, C. (2022). From adjustment to structural changes – Innovation activity of enterprises in the time of COVID-19 pandemic. *Innovation: The European Journal of Social Science Research*, *37*(4), 900–925. https://doi.org/10.1080/13511610.2022.2036951

Yeung, H. W. (2019). Rethinking mechanism and process in the geographical analysis of uneven development. *Dialogues in Human Geography*, *9*(3), 226–255. https://doi.org/10.1177/2043820619861861

Yongsheng, X., Xiaole, Z., & Wei, W. (2021). Coupling or lock-in? Co-evolution of cultural embeddness and cluster innovation-exploratory case study of Shaoxing textile cluster. *Technology in Society*, *67*, 101765. https://doi.org/10.1016/j.techsoc.2021.101765

Zhao, L., Liang, Y., & Tu, H. (2023). How do clusters drive firm performance in the regional innovation system? A causal complexity analysis in Chinese strategic emerging industries. *Systems*, *11*(5), 229. https://doi.org/10.3390/systems11050229

Zukauskaite, E., Trippl, M., & Plechero, M. (2017). Institutional thickness revisited. *Economic Geography*, *93*(4), 325–345. https://doi.org/10.1080/00130095.2017.1331703

2 Energy Clusters in Multiscalar Energy Policy

2.1 The Essence and Legal Basis of Energy Clusters

The Key Properties and Definition of Energy Clusters

An energy cluster can be thought of as a special case of a cluster concept, adapted to the purposes of economic policy. In Polish legislation, the definitional and economic scope of this project is regulated by the current version of the *Act of February 20, 2015 on Renewable Energy Sources*, amended in 2024. In Article 2(15a), the referred law defines an energy cluster as an agreement in the area of cooperation in the generation, storage, demand balancing, distribution, or trading of electricity or fuels, or heat, in order to provide its parties with economic, social, or environmental benefits or to increase flexibility of the power system (Polish Journal of Laws of 2024, item 1361). According to the latest amendment of 2024, an energy cluster includes at least a local government unit or a capital company established by a local government unit, or a capital company that owns at least 50% of the shares in a local government company (Polish Journal of Laws of 2024, item 1361). Changes to Polish legislation significantly affecting energy clusters were not preceded by further amendments until late 2023.

According to the respective Act amended in 2024, an energy cluster covers at most the area of one county or five municipalities and operates only within the borders of one country, which determines the location and geographical restrictions of the implementation of such a project. Additionally, members of the energy cluster are connected to the distribution network of the same operator of the power distribution system with a rated voltage less than 110 kV (Polish Journal of Laws of 2024, item 1361). Such a definition of the energy cluster in the legislation gives an opportunity to expand the cluster's area of operation. It allows for an increase in the competitiveness of the region, dynamic development of infrastructure, the possibility of giving land for investments, and, consequently, launching innovative enterprises in close proximity and increasing the diversity of services provided (Kupiec, 2020).

DOI: 10.4324/9781003623540-3

Another approach to the definition of the energy cluster has been proposed in the joint project entitled *The concept of the functioning of energy clusters in Poland*, implemented by the National Energy Conservation Agency, WiseEuropa, Atmoterm, and the National Institute for Distributed Energy (National Energy Conservation Agency et al., 2017). According to this expert report, an energy cluster is an agreement concluded in writing, under pain of nullity, for the purpose of joint and coordinated balancing of the supply and demand for energy or gaseous fuels in a given area through activities in the field of their generation, distribution, or trading, which at the same time appoints a coordinator of the energy cluster (National Energy Conservation Agency et al., 2017). Therefore, an energy cluster should be considered in terms of a new model within the already existing energy market in a given region, which is regulated by the distribution system operator (Kupiec, 2020). It follows that the energy cluster is not obliged to create its own energy infrastructure, which is difficult, or even impossible, especially in the initial phase of its development, and should instead cooperate with the microgrid power system (Mataczyńska, 2017).

A microgrid represents a locally controlled cluster of facilities that operate in-grid and off-grid, that is, in a partly autonomous manner against the traditional centralized grid (Marnay et al., 2012). The energy cluster and the microgrid are highly coupled to each other and, based on this symbiosis, a local energy community emerges. Energy communities are often treated as synonymous with energy clusters, and in this book, we use both terms interchangeably, together with such expressions as energy cluster initiatives or energy cluster organizations (Lis & Lis, 2021, 2023). Energy clusters form an environment within which producers and consumers operate to balance the demand for energy (Mataczyńska, 2017). Therefore, an energy cluster should demonstrate reliability in terms of technical requirements and continuity of energy supply (Mataczyńska, 2017).

Regarding governance arrangements, the cluster coordinator represents the members of the agreement (Polish Journal of Laws of 2024, item 1361). Moreover, the coordinator of the energy cluster is responsible for the organization of the cluster in the institutional sphere and for reconciling the interests of the cluster members in the area of operations and strategic development (National Energy Conservation Agency et al., 2017). The competences of the coordinator also include the preparation of a cluster's energy balance and to initiate investment in the construction of new energy generation sources (Energy Market Information Centre, 2018). Furthermore, the coordinator should seek the opportunities for innovation development through a cooperation with research centers and institutions providing research and development (R&D)-related financial support (Mataczyńska, 2017). The role of the cluster coordinator also consists of promoting ecological goals (Energy Market Information Centre, 2018).

Energy Clusters in Polish Legislation

The Polish legal system, the functioning of energy clusters is regulated by the provisions of the *Act of February 20, 2015 on Renewable Energy Sources*, after the amendment of 2024, which in Article 2(15a) defines the legal and spatial aspects (Polish Journal of Laws of 2024, item 1361). Additionally, for the energy cluster's responsibilities in innovation and R&D activities, the provisions of the *Act of July 20, 2018 – Law on Higher Education and Science* are relevant to specify the research units as potential collaborators (Polish Journal of Laws of 2022, item 574 amended). Given that the activity of an energy cluster is closely linked to local governments, we should also point at the provisions of the *Act of June 5, 1998 on County Self-Government* (Polish Journal of Laws 1998 No. 91 item 578) and *Act of March 8, 1990 on Municipal Self-Government* (Polish Journal of Laws 1990 No. 16 item 95). Ultimately, the *Act of April 10, 1997 on Energy Law* (Polish Journal of Laws 1997 No. 54 item 348) defines the principles of the country's energy policy as a framework for the rationale and operations of energy clusters.

With regard to legal forms, energy clusters act as public-private partnerships, which are regulated by the *Act of December 19, 2008 on Public-Private Partnership*. This legal act defines the public-private partnership as a joint implementation of a project based on the division of tasks and risks between the public and private parties (Polish Journal of Laws 2009 No. 19 item 100). The Act affects the rules of the cluster's cooperation with local governments, such as municipalities, communes, and counties.

We also need to recognize the importance of the *Act of May 20, 2016 on Energy Efficiency*. It defines the tasks of public sector entities in the field of energy efficiency and energy savings (Polish Journal of Laws 2016, item 831). Furthermore, it specifies the scope of tasks assigned to local governments, including the implementation and financing of projects aimed at improving energy efficiency and the purchase of equipment, installations, or vehicles featuring low energy consumption and low operating costs (Polish Journal of Laws 2016, item 831). As local government units are legally required to maintain energy security in the region, the participation of energy clusters in the implementation of these tasks is fully justified.

Other laws and documents that affect the operations of energy clusters have been specified in the project entitled *The concept of the functioning of energy clusters in Poland*, commissioned by the Ministry of Energy (National Energy Conservation Agency et al., 2017). In Table 2.1, we highlight the most crucial acts.

Energy Clusters in European Union Legislation

As a member state, Poland is obliged to implement and adapt to the provisions of EU law, such as Directive 2012/27/EU of the European Parliament and of the EU Council of October 25, 2012. The directive *emphasizes the objectives*

Table 2.1 Legislation on energy clusters

Legislation	*Official journal designation*
Act of September 15, 2000. Commercial Companies Code	*Polish Journal of Laws of 2000. No. 94, item 1037, as amended.*
Corporate Income Tax Act of February 15, 1992	*Polish Journal of Laws of 1992. No. 21, item 86, as amended.*
Act of May 20, 2016 on Energy Efficiency	*Polish Journal of Law 2016, item 831*
Act of August 27, 2009 on Public Finance	*Polish Journal of Laws of 2009. No. 157, item 1240, as amended.*
Act of December 18, 2016 on Foundations	*Polish Journal of Laws of 2015, item 40*
Act of October 26, 2000 on Commodity Exchanges	*Polish Journal of Laws of 2000. No. 103, item 1099, as amended.*
Act of December 20, 1996 on Municipal Management	*Polish Journal of Laws of 1997. No. 9, item 43, as amended.*
Act of August 21, 1997 on Real Estate Management	*Polish Journal of Laws 1997 No. 115 item 741*
The Renewable Energy Sources Act of February 20, 2015 as amended in 2024	*Polish Journal of Laws 2024, item 1361*
Act on Local Taxes and Fees of May 6, 2016	*Polish Journal of Law 2016, item 716*
Personal Income Tax Act of July 26, 1991	*Polish Journal of Laws of 1991. No. 80, item 350, as amended.*
Forest Tax Act of March 11, 2016	*Polish Journal of Law 2016, item 374*
Agricultural Tax Act of April 19, 2016	*Polish Journal of Laws of 2016, item 617*
Act of March 8, 1990 on Municipal Self-Government	*Polish Journal of Laws. 1990 No. 16 item 95*
Act of June 5, 1998 on County Local Government	*Polish Journal of Law 2016, item 814*
Act of June 5, 1998 on the Local Government of the Province	*Polish Journal of Laws 1998 No. 91 item 576*
Act of July 2, 2004 on Freedom of Economic Activity	*Polish Journal of Laws of 2004. No. 173, item 1807, as amended.*
Act of March 11, 2004 on Tax on Goods and Services	*Polish Journal of Laws of 2004. No. 54, item 535, as amended.*
Act of April 10, 1997 on Energy Law	*Polish Journal of Laws 1997 No. 54 item 348*
Act of April 7, 1989, Law on Associations	*Polish Journal of Laws of 1989. No. 20, item 104, as amended.*
Act of September 16, 1982, Cooperative Law	*Polish Journal of Laws of 1982. No. 30, item 210, as amended.*
Act of January 29, 2004, Public Procurement Law	*Polish Journal of Laws of 2004. No. 19, item 177, as amended.*

Source: National Energy Conservation Agency et al. (2017, pp. 9–13).

of the strategy for employment and smart, long-term economic growth taking into account social inclusion for all Member States of the European Union (European Parliament, 2012). This document has been reflected in Polish legislation in the Act on energy efficiency (National Energy Conservation Agency et al., 2017). Furthermore, the directions of cluster development are proposed in the *Communication from the Commission to the European Parliament, the Council of the European Economic and Social Committee and the Committee of the Regions of 2014*, whereby the European Commission recommends the creation of smart specialization areas using the framework of regional and industrial policies (European Commission, 2014).

The innovative nature of regional clusters makes them crucial to competitive advantages not only in domestic but also foreign markets. The European Commission (2014) also recommends fostering innovative solutions and promoting small and medium-sized enterprises as important tenants of clusters. In order to achieve these objectives, it is crucial to ensure value-added chains, starting from the supply of raw materials to their effective use in the production process and subsequent distribution of finished products. The European Commission proposes to upgrade traditional production methods with new technologies (European Commission, 2014). Clusters can also create the advantages of effective supply management (Golarz, 2016).

The provisions of the Directive of the European Parliament and of the Council of December 11, 2018 on the promotion of the use of energy from renewable sources (EU 2018/2001) are also in force in Poland. The directive states that the increased use of energy from renewable sources is crucial for the implementation of climate and energy policy until 2030, assuming emission reductions by at least 40% compared to 1990 (L 328/82). Article 3(1) of the same Directive also declares the achievement of 32% of renewable sources in total gross energy consumption by the end of 2030 (L 328/105). The provisions of the directive provide incentives to systematically limit other than renewable energy sources (RESs) to ensure zero-emission methods of energy production. Consequently, in Polish law, clusters are assumed to generate energy from renewable sources or from other sources or fuels (Polish Journal of Laws 2024, item 1361). The respective regulations significantly affect the operations of enterprises dependent on traditional energy sources. This, in turn, requires that national energy market regulators govern energy transformation in a thoughtful and responsible manner and with the adoption of modern technologies (Krzywicka & Żebrowska, 2020).

2.2 Energy Clusters and Cluster-Based Policies

Energy Clusters in Polish Policy Directions

There is no coherent national cluster policy that would specify the operations and support of clusters in Poland. Cluster policy is not a separate policy area but is included in other policies, such as economic, energy, infrastructure, and innovation policies. The formulation of cluster policies belongs to the regional level of government rather than to the national level (Szultka, 2012). However, the fragmentation of cluster policy within individual regions and local governments can lead to the growth of already wealthy centers and deepen uneven regional development and income disparities (Kłos & Szymańczak, 2014). In the context of energy clusters, the outflow of companies from poorer regions and the concentration in richer locations can affect energy poverty, understood as unmet essential energy requirements within one's residence at an affordable cost (Boguszewski & Herudziński, 2018). Therefore, a nationwide strategy for supporting energy clusters is needed to avoid these threats (National Energy Conservation Agency et al., 2017).

Regarding the territorial specificity of energy clusters, their local scope was not changed in the latest legal amendments, and these energy communities are treated as one of the basic elements of local policy (Polish Journal of Laws of 2024, item 1361). However, the amendment referred to, active from 2024, includes the shift in the recommended membership structure. Before the 2023–2024 amendments, an energy cluster was understood as a civil law agreement, which may include natural persons, legal persons, scientific entities, research institutes, or local government units (Polish Journal of Laws 2015, item 478). According to the latest amendment, a party to the cluster agreement is at least a local government unit or a capital company established by a local government unit, or a capital company that owns at least 50% of shares in a local government company (Polish Journal of Laws of 2024, item 1361).

Within the national-level cluster policies, three evolutionary stages can be identified. *The first phase* falls in 2004–2006 and was driven by Poland's accession to the European Union in 2004. Upon the accession, not only a stream of structural funds flowed into the country but also European measures to promote the integration of enterprises within cluster structures (Citkowski, 2020). *The second phase* in the formulation of cluster policies took place in the years 2007–2013 and was marked by attempts to include the idea of clustering in the Polish economic strategy. This resulted in the creation of an increased number of cluster initiatives, which exceeded 50 units (Citkowski, 2020). The rise in new cluster initiatives was a response to the post-crisis reality as indicated in the Commission's 2010 Communication, entitled *Europe 2020: A strategy for smart, sustainable, and inclusive growth* (European Commission, 2010). The respective Strategy has influenced the promotion and rooting of clusters in the European Union (EU) reality. The priorities of the Europe 2020 strategy included i) smart growth understood as based on knowledge and innovation (*smart growth*), ii) sustainable development of the economy with responsible and efficient use of natural resources (*sustainable growth*), and

iii) development that supports social inclusion and a high-employment economy (*inclusive growth*) (Grądziel, 2014). *The third phase* of national cluster policies took place in the years 2014–2020 and was characterized by the professionalization of management in existing initiatives to seek the status of a national lead cluster. Cluster certification processes were initiated to identify the top initiatives and recognize them as Key National Clusters with a potential for international expansion (Citkowski, 2020). The objectives of the cluster policies were not equally met in all regions and local communities. Therefore, it is important to strengthen coordination activities in this policy implementation. However, it must be admitted that coordination represents a weakness of cluster policy, in particular at the regional level (Citkowski, 2020).

Despite the lack of a well-coordinated cluster strategy, there are regions which actively develop and engage clusters in public tasks in accordance with the provisions of the *Act of April 24, 2003 on Public Benefit Activities and Volunteering* (Polish Journal of Laws 2003 No. 96 item 873). The provisions of Article 4, paragraph 1 of the respective Act define the scope of public tasks and set out the format of public-private partnership in this area. Points 11–14 of the Act identify the activities potentially implemented by clusters, such as supporting the development of entrepreneurship, creativity and innovation, the development of local communities, science, and higher education (Polish Journal of Laws 2003 No. 96 item 873).

Energy Clusters in European Union Policy Directions

The European Commission posits that economic development based on a modern cluster policy is an effective trajectory for productive growth of enterprises and society well-being (European Commission, 2016). The condition and potential of the country's economy are increasingly linked to smart specialization strategies, which lead to economic transformation and competitive advantages in well-defined priority areas (European Commission, 2016). An indispensable element of modern cluster policy is innovation, dependent on new technologies and qualified human resources (Frias et al., 2020). The European Commission places clusters, including energy clusters, as one of the foundations for improving production efficiency and the use of new technologies, which drive the growth of companies and increase social welfare (European Commission, 2016).

Energy Clusters in Regional Policy Directions

The European Commission emphasizes the uniqueness of spatial conditions and localization economies as drivers of cluster development (European Commission, 2016). The place-based policy assumes that there is no one universal path of development, and it is impossible to plan a uniform cluster development strategy for all EU member states. Regions differ in wealth and development and natural conditions; therefore, each of them should implement an individual cluster policy, adapting it to economic realities and using comparative advantages from specialization (Szczepaniak, 2018).

Clusters constitute a well-functioning market environment for companies, which cannot be achieved out of these specialized agglomerations. Efficient economic governance in clusters removes the need for public intervention, including antitrust policy (Kosiński, 2004). Therefore, governments should allocate resources to cluster development to increase the competitiveness and innovation of enterprises and to avoid market failure (European Commission, 2016). Ultimately, cooperation between the public and private sectors should be strengthened and cluster-based policy should be treated as a bridge between the state and entrepreneurs (European Commission, 2016).

Clusters, including energy clusters, due to their spatial boundaries, are one of the foundations for the development of regional development policy, focusing on the growth of entrepreneurship and innovation. An example of this development policy can be found in the Małopolska region, where scientific potential of highly developed universities and research centers benefits clusters and technology parks operating in knowledge-based industries (Grądziel, 2014). Based on the knowledge exchanges between academia and business, clusters stimulate new venture creation, increase the region's competitive advantage, and attract foreign investment (Grycuk, 2010).

Energy Clusters in Energy Policy Directions

Energy clusters are also the foundation of energy policy, the main goal of which has been to ensure the country's energy security (Stępień, 2011). Considering limited and exhausted sources of non-renewable energy, it is important to support innovations in the area of renewable sources (Ruszel & Pomiotko, 2019). Moreover, climate changes not only adversely affects the natural environment, but also pose a threat to economic development (Masson-Delmotte et al., 2021). The focus on continuous gross domestic product (GDP) growth determines the increasing dependence on energy-intensive production. Consequently, countries rich in energy sources are gaining an advantage in the international arena, dictating their conditions on the global commodity markets (Ruszel & Pomiotko, 2019). The geopolitical game of superpowers may effectively limit the economic growth of countries that do not adjust to their international policy or oppose their expansion. Power differences can even lead to the paralysis of economies that are excessively dependent on energy supplies if countries rich in energy sources abandon further distribution and contract fulfillment.

Therefore, it is necessary to base energy policy on reliable domestic energy producers that can ensure energy security regardless of the geopolitical situation and potential crises caused by the interruption of supply chains (Okraszewska, 2016). In 2010, several strategic actions were taken within the European community to reduce the level of electricity consumption by the member states and increase R&D expenditures (Gronkowska, 2017). The "Fit for 55" package, as part of the European Green Deal, is relevant for energy cluster development. The document follows the assumptions of the Paris Agreement, emphasizing not only aspirations but obligations of the member states in this regard (European Commission, 2021). As the European Commission underlines, the implementation of the "Fit for 55" package is not only about moving toward climate neutrality with the use of new energy-focused technologies, but also to reduce energy poverty, implement innovative activities, and create new jobs (European Commission, 2021).

The institutional framework provided by the EU set out a comprehensive grounding for the creation of new clusters and the upgradation of existing ones. Energy initiatives are assigned a crucial role in fulfilling the assumptions of the European Green Deal and in solving many economic problems. The latter range from active participation in the energy transition to the creation of innovative solutions, to the organization of the regional labor market, and to increasing economic efficiency through the local balance of energy demand (Fraś & Ivashchuk, 2017). Energy clusters enhance the energy potential of the region due to their spatial proximity to local enterprises and households. The location of energy-generating devices in close proximity to end users allows one to avoid losses related to distribution and transmission costs that increase with distance (Lovins, 1976). Energy clusters can also respond appropriately to the demand for energy at a given time, thus avoiding problems of overproduction and incorrect forecasting of energy demand in the future (Lovins, 1976).

However, the role of energy clusters in energy policy is not only in addressing energy demand and energy production but also in promoting RES. This role is emphasized in the document *Responsible Development Strategy*, adopted in 2017 by the Polish Council of Ministers, where stable RES are promoted concurrently with the development of energy clusters and cooperatives (Supreme Audit Office, 2017). Distributed energy, being one of the domains of energy democracy, has become a foundation for ensuring the energy security (Okraszewska, 2016). The essence of distributed energy is the dispersion of sources, that is, their physical location in many places and their proximity to energy consumers, allowing more efficient energy use and balance (Ministry of Development and Technology, 2025). Distributed energy is enhanced by RES, including the energy from wind, solar, aerothermal, geothermal, hydrothermal, hydropower, wave, current, tidal, ambient, biomass, biogas, agricultural biogas, biomethane, bioliquids, and renewable hydrogen sources (Polish Journal of Laws of 2024, item 1361).

Distributed energy balances the demand for energy when there are interruptions in supply due to grid failures or capacity limitations (Popczyk, 2011). According to Statistics Poland, in 2023, the share of renewable energy in gross final energy consumption was 16.5% (Statistics Poland, 2024). In turn, the Energy Regulatory Office provides data on the installed capacity of RESs in Poland, where, as of June 30, 2024, there was almost 33 GW (gigawatts) of capacity in all technologies (Energy Regulatory Office, 2025a).

Clusters are catalysts for innovative solutions to meet the environmental requirements set by both national and EU legislators (Kowalczyk-Juśko, 2021). Energy policy, innovation policy, and environmental protection policy can meet these requirements by developing energy clusters. The integration of the respective policies is necessary to achieve the intended zero-emission economy within all member states of the EU (Popczyk, 2011). This goal is considered paramount by European decision makers and has also been included in *Poland's Strategy for Responsible Development* focusing on energy transition (Ministry of Development, 2017). However, this large-scale undertaking cannot only be achieved by spending dedicated EU funds, but also requires close cooperation from the public and private sectors to go through this process in an effective manner.

Regarding the context of the EU's energy policy, in 2020, a Regulation of the European Parliament and the Council established the Just Transition Fund under cohesion policy for 2021–2027. The fund aims to achieve a low-carbon economy in Europe, acknowledging the principles of a just energy transition (European Commission, 2020). Implementing these activities in the context of the national energy policy should be based on mutual trust of the private sector and public institutions and thus on exchange and access to full information, allowing effective financing of eco-innovative and pro-ecological activities (Brzezowska-Borcz, 2019).

Ultimately, the implementation of the objectives of energy policy at the EU and national levels is strongly linked to the objectives of other policies, especially the sustainable development policy. However, the latter policy is not purely local or regional, but is an idea spread on a global scale. Therefore, clusters in this approach will no longer pursue only the goals of individual countries but will support a much broader idea.

2.3 Local Energy Communities in Sustainable Development Policy

The Essence of Sustainable Development Policy

The concept and policy for sustainable development are most precisely reflected in the Report of the World Commission on Environment and Development from 1987, entitled *Our common future*, which sets out the United Nations (UN) General Assembly to *A global agenda of change* (UN, 1987). This document calls for the implementation of a long-term environmental strategy, which assumed the achievement of sustainable development by the year 2000 and the years following this period; strengthening cooperation between developed and developing countries in social and economic spheres; searching for ways and obtaining funds to support environmental protection in the international dimension; and defining a long-term perception of environmental issues and the related long-term recovery program (UN, 1987).

The idea of sustainable development promotes environmental integrity and creates conditions for further development (Pujer, 2016). Radical advocates of the natural environment place it above anthropocentric interests (Rogall, 2010). However, the sustainable approach does not ignore wider social needs and seek to reconcile biocentric and anthropocentric positions. The aim is primarily to reduce the negative impact of excessive consumerism on the balance of the natural environment, while looking for pro-ecological solutions and technologies (Pujer, 2016). Hence, the efforts to involve social and economic actors in shaping the growth trajectory.

Another document that sets the goals of sustainable development policy is the resolution adopted by 193 member states within the framework of the General Assembly of the UN on September 25, 2015. The document contains 17 Sustainable Development Goals (SDGs) and 169 tasks related to the economic, social, and environmental dimensions (UN, 2015). Among them, there are tasks suitable for energy clusters, such as reducing energy poverty and enabling access to clean energy, improving the quality of education and increasing the level of innovation of the economy, and equalizing opportunities (UNIC Warsaw, 2016).

Given the social, economic, and environmental issues raised in the public debate, the implementation of the objective of the sustainable development policy rests on several policy areas, which can cause some misunderstandings at the decision-making level. Therefore, stronger coordination is needed within the framework of sustainable development policy, to involve governments, international organizations, business entities, and the civil society at large (UN, 2015).

Energy Clusters as a Foundation for Achieving Sustainable Development Policy Goals

The activities of energy clusters are conducive to reducing the level of water, land, and air pollution, and to the achievement of climate neutrality by 2050 (Kulik et al., 2020). Therefore, clusters pursue multiple goals, from the implementation of the provisions of the national and EU-level energy policy to promotion of distributed energy and increase in energy efficiency (Kulik et al., 2020; Rolbiecki, 2015). Cluster initiatives can serve as an instrument for place-based adaptation of policies (Derlukiewicz et al., 2020). Clusters can operate at many levels and constitute a bridge between various types of institutions from the public, private, and scientific sectors around a clear area of specialization

(Pujer, 2016). Moreover, clusters feature agglomeration of specialized entities, which gives an advantage over dispersed industrial structures (Pujer, 2016). Specialization and a common competence base allow prioritization and targeting of policy instruments to the unique needs of these agglomerations. These processes are especially evident in emerging industries, which require customized investments in technology and human resources (Pujer, 2016).

The potential generated by energy clusters is strengthened due to linking the goals and efforts of companies and local governments (Derlukiewicz et al., 2020). As part of this symbiosis, social trust is also built not only in local governments, but also in local enterprises, which can perform tasks commissioned by local authorities, as well as gain their acceptance and financial support (Pujer, 2016). Furthermore, energy clusters exert influence on social changes towards a collaborative approach to sustainable goals and improved social capital and human resource competencies (Rudzewicz, 2016). A qualified and collaborative workforce translates into an increase in the level of competitiveness of the region and determines the strength of the cluster's advantage over dispersed enterprises. In addition, a region with an attractive labor market prevents economic migration (Górny & Kaczmarczyk, 2003). In summary, clusters can lead to eliminating income gaps, preventing economic and energy poverty, and reducing the problem of social inequalities (Kalinowska-Nawrotek, 2004; Nadvi & Barrientos, 2004).

A crucial focus of cluster policy is also to increase interest in innovative activities and knowledge transfer between cluster members and business environment institutions (Derlukiewicz et al., 2020). Clusters, as industrial agglomerations, can achieve faster and better results in these areas than companies operating alone. Due to the capital intensity of technological projects, enterprises organized within a cluster structure can cofinance their R&D activities and receive support from local governments as part of the public-private partnership (Pujer, 2016). At this point, it is also worth looking at the discussed structures through the prism of incubators for innovations, which have the ability to implement eco-innovations, often referred to as sustainable development innovations (Strojny et al., 2010). Additionally, the activities of clusters, especially those of an eco-innovative nature, have a positive impact on the quality of life of residents within a given location (Pujer, 2016). Hence, we observe an intersection of activities that involve technical progress and environmental protection (Strojny et al., 2010).

A condition for this activity is the active pursuit of R&D activity and dissemination of knowledge, as well as the participation of research units in the development of new technologies. One of the elements of sustainable development policy is the dissemination of the idea of science as a strategic resource that determines the strength and pace of development of the knowledge-based economy (Pujer, 2016). In this case, knowledge is a strategic resource of the cluster (Bembenek, 2012). In addition to the integration of entrepreneurial and research environments, mutual trust, promotion of cooperation, and a growing importance of socially responsible business can emerge (Żychlewicz, 2015). Furthemore, a cluster organization is responsible for promoting sustainability ideas among other market participants (Crowther & Aras, 2008). From this perspective, clusters not only promote knowledge about the use of new technologies, but can also have a real impact on building social awareness.

On the basis of the above discussion of individual sustainable development goals and their relationships with the cluster phenomenon, it can be concluded that the requests assigned to clusters allow one to fulfill local government responsibilities and needs of enterprises. The expected contribution of the energy clusters to achieving the objectives of the sustainable development policy is presented in Table 2.2.

Table 2.2 Contribution of energy clusters to individual dimensions of sustainable development policy

	Dimensions of sustainable development policy		
	Economic	*Social*	*Environmental*
Contribution of energy clusters	Increase in the level of innovation, equalizing opportunities within the regions; increasing the competitiveness of regions (country), increasing interest in innovative activities and knowledge transfer between cluster members and business environment institutions, dissemination of knowledge and participation of research units in activities in the field of new technologies	Reduction of poverty levels (including energy poverty), improving the quality of education, increase in the quality of social capital, eliminating income gaps, preventing economic poverty, reducing the problem of social inequalities, and wage discrimination	Access to clean energy that complies with pollutant emission standards, increasing the share of eco-innovation in industry, improving living conditions thanks to the improved state of the environment, reducing the exploitation of fossil fuels, improving the quality of the natural environment

Sources: own elaboration based on Crowther and Aras (2008); Kalinowska-Nawrotek (2004); Nadvi and Barrientos (2004); Strojny et al. (2010); Pujer (2016); Rudzewicz (2016); UNIC Warsaw (2016); National Energy Conservation Agency et al. (2017); Derlukiewicz et al. (2020).

2.4 Institutional Framework for Energy Clusters in Poland

Institutions Supporting the Development of Energy Clusters

The first mentions of cluster initiatives in the Polish public space took place in the second half of the 1990s. However, the structures in question became apparent after Poland joined the EU in 2004, and the projects that supported cluster creation were firmly established in strategic regional development plans (Kraska, 2018). However, Polish legislation has acknowledged energy clusters only since 2016, as part of subsequent amendments of the Act of February 20, 2015 on Renewable Energy Sources, where only one article has been dedicated to the legal definition of the cluster (Polish Journal of Laws of 2015, item 478). On the other hand, energy cooperatives have been given much more space in the provisions of the same Act because they are a focus of 13 articles. What follows is that energy clusters in the Polish legal system have been neglected to some extent (Mataczyńska & Kucharska, 2020). This is surprising given their important role in the implementation of energy policy and ensuring energy security in regions, countries, and the entire community, as discussed in the legal acts and policy documents above (European Commission, 2014).

Despite the lack of precision on the nature of energy clusters in the legal and policy frameworks, numerous business models have been adopted to establish energy initiatives and introduce them to the local energy market (Mataczyńska & Kucharska, 2020). Moreover, it is important to note the institutions founded to support the development of clusters, including the Ministry for Climate and Environment, the Ministry of Economy, the Ministry of Development and Technology, the Ministry of Science and Higher Education, the Polish Agency for Enterprise Development, and the Industrial Development Agency (Kraska, 2018). The Ministry of Energy is undoubtedly the main body in the formation and functioning of cluster initiatives (Tauron Polska Energia, 2024).

The operations of these initiatives are also influenced by the President of the Energy Regulatory Office. This office verifies the concession requirements (National Energy Conservation Agency et al., 2017) and appoints a distribution network operator in accordance with Article 9 of the *Energy Law* (Polish Journal of Laws 1997 No. 54 item 348). The Energy Regulatory Office rules the energy sector and maintains a register of energy clusters in the Public Information Bulletin, based on applications from the energy cluster coordinators.

The coordinator of the energy cluster entered in the register is obliged to prepare annual reports, including information on the energy generated with an emphasis from RES and installed capacity in RES, energy storage facilities. In the respective Energy Law document, only one article has been dedicated to the legal definition facilities of the cluster owned by the cluster members (Polish Journal of Laws of 2015, item 478). The cluster registration process is in the nascent stage, and only six energy clusters formalized their membership in the respective register in 2024 (Energy Regulatory Office, 2025b). This may be evidence of little attention and monitoring devoted to these important actors in the energy sector. The strategic document *Polish Energy Policy until 2040* indicates only 66 energy clusters in 2020, while 300 entities are expected to do so by 2030 (Ministry of Climate and Environment, 2021).

Undoubtedly, preferential conditions regarding distribution fees would act as an incentive for the creation of new energy clusters and their entry into the formal register. According to Article 184k. of the *Renewable Energy Sources Act* amended in 2024, until December 31, 2029, no RES fee shall be charged or collected from the members of the energy cluster in relation to the amount of electricity generated from RES by the members of an energy cluster that has been entered in the register of energy clusters and fed into the electricity distribution network, and then withdrawn from that network for consumption by the members of that energy cluster for a given hour of the settlement period. Furthermore, depending on the size of the electricity production from RES that is introduced into the electricity distribution network by the cluster members, they can count on a reduction of the distribution fee by up to 25%, if 100% of the energy consumed comes from RES. In the least favorable scenario, the fee reduction is 5%, when the threshold of 60% of the energy consumed from RES is exceeded (Polish Journal of Laws of 2024, item 1361). However, under the amended regulations active from 2024, these preferential settlements can be used by clusters formally registered until December 31, 2026, after meeting three conditions. Firstly, the cluster is required to generate and supply at the distribution network at least 30% of RES electricity. Second, the total installed electrical capacity of the RES installation and other energy-generating units in the cluster does not exceed 150 MW (megawatts). Third, the cluster enables the annual coverage of no less than 40% of the total annual electricity demand of its members, and the total installed electrical capacity of its energy storage facilities amounts to at least 2% of the total installed capacity of RES installations and other units generating energy (Polish Journal of Laws of 2024, item 1361).

On the other hand, from January 1, 2027, until December 31, 2029, the above requirements are tightened, and, regarding the first condition, the generation and introduction of electricity to the distribution network from RES should be at least 50%. Regarding the second condition, the RES should meet no less than 50% of the annual demand. Furthermore, the third condition requires that energy storage must account for at least 5% of the total installed capacity of the RES installation and other units generating energy (Polish Journal of Laws of 2015, item 478).

Institutions Financing the Development of Energy Clusters

In Poland, the main source of funding for clusters, including energy clusters, are the EU funds, in particular, the funds from the European Regional Development Fund (ERDF), which finances not only the clusters themselves, but also cooperating units. Another important source is the European Social Fund (ESF), which places a strong emphasis on increasing the quality of human and social capital (Kraska, 2018). At the same time, funds are available not only to cluster organizations, but also to entities that cooperate with clusters, that is, enterprises, business environment institutions, local government units, and representatives of R&D units (Kraska, 2018). Furthermore, clusters can benefit from the country-level Innovative Economy Operational Program, the Human Capital Operational Program, and the Regional Operational Programs dedicated to individual regions (Kraska, 2018). Energy clusters can also apply for funding from the Just Transition Fund under the 2021–2027 cohesion policy. There are also funding opportunities from the National Recovery and Resilience Plan of the Recovery and Resilience Facility (RRF), which is a part of the Recovery Plan for Europe (Ministry of Development and Technology, 2023). Ultimately, income from the cluster's activities, member fees, and own funds of the cluster participants complete the sources of financing (National Energy Conservation Agency et al., 2017).

Energy Cluster Contract Agreements

When discussing the institutional framework of energy clusters, it is also important to recognize the nature of contracting between the participants of this governance form and the types of contracts between the cluster and external entities. However, it is virtually unfeasible to classify the types of contracts due to a broad definition of the energy cluster as an agreement the subject of which is just cooperation (Polish Journal of Laws 2015, item 478). This definition does not specify the nature of the cooperation referred to. Therefore, it is impossible to propose the same contract model for participants for cluster transactions with other market participants. Energy clusters are relatively new subjects in the Polish economic and legislative framework, and there is limited experience in this regard. The energy clusters were classified by law only in 2016, which still leaves room for further exploration of this issue (Mataczyńska & Kucharska, 2020). However, several types of internal and external agreements can be identified between energy clusters. The types of agreements are presented in Table 2.3.

The Role of the Energy Cluster Coordinator

This list of types of contracts does not exhaust the entire catalog of documents that can be signed with the cluster or as part of the cluster's operations. Within

Table 2.3 Types of contracts applied by energy clusters

Types of contracts	
Internal	*External*
The agreement of the energy cluster constituting its establishment (includes, e.g., the purpose of the establishment; the parties to the agreement; the subject of the action; the obligation to appoint the cluster coordinator; the territorial scope).	Distribution service agreement pursuant to Article 5 of the Energy Law (Polish Journal of Laws of 1997 No. 54, Item 348).
Energy sale agreement on the basis of Article 5 of the Energy Law (Polish Journal of Laws of 1997 No. 54, item 348).	Agreement for the provision of external services.
Sales and distribution agreement between the cluster coordinator and the cluster members.	Agreement for the sale of energy between the cluster coordinator and customers who are not members of the respective cluster.

Sources: National Energy Conservation Agency, WiseEuropa, Atmoterm, and National Institute for Distributed Energy (2017).

this contracting schema, the role of the energy cluster coordinator reapers is crucial. Although the coordinator of the energy cluster is indicated in the RES Act, the legislator mainly emphasizes its representative nature (Polish Journal of Laws 2015, item 478). In the Polish legislation, the cluster coordinator has received little attention, and this calls for more clarification of its functions, the more that this entity performs more tasks than merely a representative function. The cluster coordinator primarily manages the operations of the cluster, which includes rating energy and balancing energy demand within the cluster, coordinating fuel supplies from contractors, engaging local fuel producers to cooperate with the cluster, and operating an internal distribution system. Furthermore, the coordinator sets the development strategy of the cluster, cooperates with research units initiating innovative activities, monitors investment processes within the cluster, and raises external funding for further operations (National Energy Conservation Agency et al., 2017). This list of tasks is not exhaustive, since the provision of the group's founding agreement can expand the duties of the coordinator.

Institutional Drawbacks

It is difficult to resist the impression that not enough attention has been paid to energy clusters in Poland, both in terms of legislation and institutions. First, there is a large margin of error in the interpretation of legal acts, including the *Renewable Energy Sources Act of February 20, 2015*, amended between 2023 and 2024. This law devotes only one point to the definitional nature of energy cluster initiatives. Despite the legislator's incentives, such as preferential settlement conditions for energy clusters and the benefits of being listed in the register of energy clusters, there is no systemized list of currently operating energy clusters in Poland. Information on the number of active and existing units is not monitored by any of the supervising institutions. Insufficient information and a lack of reliable records represent an obstacle to proper policy design and research focused on policy recommendations in the area of cluster establishment, operations, and development.

References

Polish Journal of Laws 1997 No. 54 item 348 (1997). *Act of April 10, 1997. Energy law*.

Polish Journal of Laws 2003 No. 96 item 873 (2023). *Act of April 24, 2003 on Public Benefit Activities and Volunteering*.

Polish Journal of Laws 2009 No. 19 item 100 (2008). *Act of December 19, 2008 on Public-Private Partnership*.

Polish Journal of Laws of 2015, item 478 (2015). *Act of February 20, 2015 on Renewable Energy Sources*.

Polish Journal of Laws of 2024, item 1361 (2024). *Act of February 20, 2015 on Renewable Energy Sources, amended in 2024*.

Polish Journal of Laws of 2022, item 574, as amended (2018). *Act of July 20, 2018. Law on Higher Education and Science*.

Polish Journal of Laws 1998 No. 91 item 578 (1998). *Act of June 5, 1998 on County Self-Government*.

Polish Journal of Laws 1990 No. 16 item 95 (1990). *Act of March 8, 1990 on Municipal Self-Government*.

Polish Journal of Laws 2016, item 831 (2016). *Act of May 20, 2016 on energy efficiency*.

Bembenek, B. (2012). *Zarządzanie wiedzą w klastrze. Zarządzanie wiedzą w klastrze. Zeszyty naukowe Uniwersytetu Szczecińskiego nr 709. Problemy zarzdząnia, finansów i marketing, 2012, no. 23.* Wydawnictwo Naukowe Uniwersytetu Szczecińskiego, Szczecin, pp. 11–26.

Boguszewski, R., & Herudziński, T. (2018). *Ubóstwo energetyczne w Polsce*. Pracownia Badań Społecznych SGGW, Warsaw.

Brzezowska-Borcz, M. (2019). *Polityka Ekologiczna Państwa 2030*. Ministry of the Environment, Warsaw.

Citkowski, M. (2020). *Kierunki rozwoju polityki klastrowej w Polsce po 2020 roku*. Ministry of Development, Innovation Department, Warsaw.

Crowther, D., & Aras, G. (2008). *Corporate social responsibility*. Ventus Publishing ApS BookBooN.com.

Derlukiewicz, N., et.al. (2020). *How do clusters foster sustainable development*? An analysis of EU policies. *Sustainability 12*(4), 1297. https://doi.org/10.3390/su12041297.

Energy Market Information Centre (2018). *Zawiązanie klastra energii to dopiero początek*. https://www.cire.pl/artykuly/materialy-problemowe/137197-zawiazanie-klastra-energii-to-dopiero-poczatek (Accessed December 28, 2024).

Energy Regulatory Office (2025a). *Instalacje odnawialnych źródeł energii - stan na 30 czerwca 2024 r.* https://www.ure.gov.pl/pl/oze/potencjal-krajowy-oze/8108,Instalacje-odnawialnych-zrodel-energii-stan-na-30-czerwca-2024-r.html (Accessed January 20, 2025).

Energy Regulatory Office (2025b). *Rejestr Klastrów Energii.* Biuletyn Informacji Publicznej. https://bip.ure.gov.pl/bip/rejestry-i-bazy/klastry/4608,Rejestr-Klastrow-Energii.html (Accessed January 2, 2025).

European Commission (2021). *'Ready for 55': Achieving the EU's 2030 climate target. On the road to climate neutrality.* Brussels, 14.7.2021. COM(2021) 550 final.

European Commission (2010). *Europe 2020. A strategy for smart, sustainable and inclusive growth.* Brussels, 3.3.2010. COM(2010) 2020 final.

European Commission (2014). *Working towards a European industrial renaissance, Communication from the Commission to the European Parliament, the Council, the European Economic and Social Committee and the Committee of the Regions.* Brussels, January 22, 2014, COM(2014) 14 final.

European Commission (2016). *Smart guide to cluster policy.* European Union.

European Commission (2020). *Proposal for a Regulation of the European Parliament and of the Council establishing the Fund for equitable transformation.*

European Parliament (2012). *DIRECTIVE 2012/27/EU OF THE EUROPEAN PARLIAMENT AND OF THE COUNCIL of October 25, 2012 on energy efficiency, amending Directives 2009/125/EC and 2010/30/EU and repealing Directives 2004/8/EC and 2006/32/EC* https://eur-lex.europa.eu/legal-content/EN/TXT/PDF/?uri=CELEX:32012L0027 (Accessed January 20, 2025).

Fraś, B., & Ivashchuk, O. (2017). *Rola klastrów w zrównoważonym rozwoju energetyki w Polsce. Polityka Energetyczna*, 2017, Vol. 20, Paper 2. Polish Academy of Sciences: www.czasopismo.pan.pl, pp. 25–40.

Frias, J., et al. (2020). *A Practitioner's Guide to Innovation Policy Instruments to Build Firm Capabilities and Accelerate Technological Catch-Up in Developing Countries.* World Bank, Washington DC. https://doi.org/10.1596/33269.

Golarz, M. (2016). *Zastosowanie metody just in time w zarządzaniu organizacją. Journal of Modern Management Process*, 2016, No, *2*(1), journalmmp.com, pp. 34–43.

Górny, A., & Kaczmarczyk, P. (2003). *Uwarunkowania i mechanizmy migracji zarobkowych w świetle wybranych koncepcji teoretycznych. Seria: „PRACE MIGRACYJNE" 2003, No. 49.* Institute of Social Studies UW, Warsaw.

Grądziel, A. (2014). *Strategia inteligentnej specjalizacji stymulatorem rozwoju gospodarczego regionów. Zeszyty Naukowe Uniwersytetu Szczecińskiego. Studia i Prace Wydziału Nauk Ekonomicznych i Zarządzania, No. 37, Vol. 2 Gospodarka regionalna i międzynarodowa.* Univeristy of Szczecin, Szczecin, pp. 243–253.

Gronkowska, J. (2017). *Polityka wsparcia tworzenia i rozwoju klastrów energii w Polsce. Zeszyty Naukowe Instytutu Gospodarki Surowcami Mineralnymi i Energią Polskiej Akademii Nauk, No. 97.* Publishing House of the Institute of Mineral and Energy Economy of the Polish Academy of Sciences, Krakow, pp. 213–230.

Grycuk, A. (2010). *Klastry jako instrument polityki regionalnej. „infos - zagadnienia społeczno-gospodarcze" No. 13(83).* Office of Parliamentary Analyses, pp. 1–4.

Kalinowska-Nawrotek, B. (2004). *Formy dyskryminacji kobiet na polskim rynku pracy. „Ruch Prawniczy, Ekonomiczny i Socjologiczny ROK LXVI", Paper 2.* Faculty of Law and Administration of Adam Mickiewicz University in Poznań, Poznań, pp. 231–245

Kłos, B., & Szymańczak, J. (2014). *Nierówności społeczne w Polsce*. Parliamentary Publishing House, Warsaw.

Kosiński, E. (2004). *Cele i instrumenty antymonopolowej interwencji państwa w gospodarkę. Kwartalnik Prawa Publicznego Year IV, No. 3/2004*. UKSW, Warsaw; TNOiK, Toruń, pp. 7–41.

Kowalczyk-Juśko, A. (2021). *Rozwój innowacyjnych technologii odnawialnych źródeł energii na obszarach wiejskich (2020)*. Agricultural Advisory Centre in Brwinów, Radom Branch, Radom.

Kraska, E. (2018). *Regionalne procesy formowania i rozwoju klastrów (na przykładzie województwa świętokrzyskiego)*. Wydawnictwo Uniwersytetu Jana Kochanowskiego, Kielce.

Krzywicka, K., & Żebrowska, A. (2020). *Transformacja energetyczna. Przyszłość zaczyna się dziś. „Future Fuelled by Knowledge"- Raport nr 13. PKN ORLEN S.A.*, Warsaw.

Kulik, O. et al. (2020). *Zeroemisyjna Polska 2050: Wrzesień 2020*. Fundacja WWF Polska. https://www.wwf.pl/ZeroemisyjnaPolska (Accessed December 12, 2024).

Kupiec, B. (2020). Analiza prawno-porównawcza klastrów energii i spółdzielni energetycznych. *„Przegląd Prawniczy Uniwersytetu Warszawskiego Rok XIX", No. 1. Faculty of Law and Administration of the University of Warsaw*, Warsaw, pp. 64–94. https://www.researchgate.net/publication/374724066_Analiza_prawno-porownawcza_klastrow_energii_i_spoldzielni_energetyeznyeh. Accessed December 25, 2024.

Lis, A. M., & Lis, A. (2021). *The cluster organization: Analyzing the development of cooperative relationships*. Routledge.

Lis, A. M., & Lis, A. (2023). *Proximity and the cluster organization*. Routledge.

Lovins, A. B. (1976). *Energy strategy: The road not taken? Foreign Affairs, 55*(1), 65–96. https://doi.org/10.2307/20039628.

Marnay, C., Zhou, N., Qu, M., & Romankiewicz, J. (2012). *International Microgrid Assessment. Governance, INcentives, and Experience, June 2012*. Ernest Orlando Lawrence, Berkeley National Laboratory. https://doi.org/10.2172/1210909

Masson-Delmotte, V., et al. (2021). *IPCC Raport. Climate Change 2021. The Physical Science Basis*. Intergovernmental Panel on Climate Change, Switzerland.

Mataczyńska, E. (2017). *Klastry energii – korzyści i szanse realizacji*. Ignacy Łukasiewicz Institute for Energy Policy, Rzeszów.

Mataczyńska, E., & Kucharska, A. (ed.). (2020). *Klastry energii: Regulacje, teoria i praktyka*. Ignacy Łukasiewicz Institute for Energy Policy, Rzeszów.

Ministry of Climate and Environment (2021). *Polityka energetyczna Polski do 2040 r*. (Ministry of Climate and Environment, Warsaw.

Ministry of Development (2017). *Strategia na rzecz Odpowiedzialnego Rozwoju do roku 2020 (z perspektywą do 2030 r.)*. Ministry of Development - Department of Development Strategies, Warsaw.

Ministry of Development and Technology (2023). *Miliony do wzięcia dla społeczności energetycznych*. https://www.gov.pl/web/rozwoj-technologia/miliony-do-wziecia-dla-spolecznosci-energetycznych (Accessed January 20, 2025).

Ministry of Development and Technology (2025). *Energetyka prosumencka i rozproszona*. https://www.gov.pl/web/rozwoj-technologia/energetyka-prosumencka-i-rozproszona (Accessed January 20, 2025)

Nadvi, K., & Barrientos, S. (2004). *Industrial clusters and poverty reduction. Towards a methodology for poverty and social impact assessment of cluster development initiatives*. United Nations Industrial Development Organization UNIDO, Vienna.

National Energy Conservation Agency, WiseEuropa-Foundation Warsaw Institute for Economic and European Studies, Atmoterm, & National Institute for Distributed Energy (2017). *Koncepcja funkcjonowania klastrów energii w Polsce*. Ministry of Energy, Warsaw.

Okraszewska, E. (2016). *Demokracja energetyczna—Społeczeństwo jako prosument energii elektrycznej. Gospodarka w Praktyce i Teorii, 43*(2), 39–50. https://doi.org/10.18778/1429-3730.43.03.

Popczyk, J. (2011). *Energetyka rozproszona: Od dominacji energetyki w gospodarce do zrównoważonego rozwoju, od paliw kopalnych do energii odnawialnej i efektywności energetycznej*. Polski Klub Ekologiczny.

Pujer, K. (ed.). (2016). *Zarządzanie organizacją w turbulentnym otoczeniu: Monografia: praca zbiorowa*. Exante, Wrocław, pp. 109–119.

Rogall, H. (2010). *Ekonomia zrównoważonego rozwoju: Teoria i praktyka*. Wydawnictwo Zysk i S-ka, Poznań.

Rolbiecki, R. (2015). *Bezpieczeństwo energetyczne unii europejskiej a polityka energetyczna w transporcie. Contemporary Economy, 6*(2), 21–32.

Rudzewicz, A. (2016). *Zaufanie społeczne w otoczeniu przedsiębiorstwa. Journal of Management and Finance 14* 203–215.

Ruszel, M., & Pomiotko, S. (Eds.). (2019). *Bezpieczeństwo energetyczne Polski i Europy: Uwarunkowania - wyzwania - innowacje*. Ignacy Lukasiewicz Institute for Energy Policy, Rzeszów.

Statistics Poland (2024). *Energia ze źródeł odnawialnych w 2023 r.* https://stat.gov.pl/download/gfx/portalinformacyjny/pl/defaultaktualnosci/5485/10/7/1/energia_ze_zrodel_odnawialnych_w_2023_r.pdf (Accessed January 20, 2025).

Stępień, J. (2011). *Metody analizy i oceny niezawodności kablowych układów zasilających średnich napięć*. Wydawnictwo Politechniki Świętokrzyskiej w Kielcach, Kielce.

Strojny, J., Wojnicka-Sycz, E., & Woźniak, L. (Eds.) (2010). *Ekoinnowacje w praktyce funkcjonowania MŚP*. Polish Agency for Enterprise Development, Warsaw.

Supreme Audit Office (2017). *Rozwój sektora odnawialnych źródeł energii—Najwyższa Izba Kontroli*. Supreme Audit Office. https://www.nik.gov.pl/kontrole/P/17/020/ (Accessed December 6, 2024).

Szczepaniak, I. (2018). *Przewagi komparatywne w handlu zagranicznym Polski na przykáadzie produktów rolno-spożywczych i pozostaáych*. Zeszyty Naukowe of the Warsaw University of Life Sciences, Warsaw, *18*(1), 263–274. https://doi.org/10.22630/PRS.2018.18.1.24.

Szultka, S. (ed.). (2012). *Klastry w Polsce—Raport z cyklu paneli dyskusyjnych*. Polish Agency for Enterprise Development, Warsaw.

Tauron Polska Energia (2024). *Klastry Energii w działaniach Ministerstwa Energii*. tauron.pl. https://www.tauron.pl/tauron/o-tauronie/tauron-dla-otoczenia/klastry-energii (Accessed December 18, 2024).

UN (1987). *Report of the World Commission on Environment and Development: Our Common Future*. http://www.ask-force.org/web/Sustainability/Brundtland-Our-Common-Future-1987-2008.pdf. Accessed December 8, 2024.

UN (2015). *Rezolucja przyjęta przez Zgromadzenie Ogólne w dniu 25 września 2015 r. Przekształcamy nasz świat: Agenda na rzecz zrównoważonego rozwoju 2030*. A/RES/70/1.

UNIC Warsaw (Ośrodek Informacji ONZ w Warszawie) (2016). *Cele Zrównoważonego Rozwoju*. un.org.pl. https://www.unic.un.org.pl/ (Accessed December 12, 2024).

3 Research Framework and Methodological Approach to Evaluating Energy Cluster Policies

3.1 Research Framework

Based on the synthesis of the literature review in Chapters 1–2, we identify the following research and policy-related gaps in knowledge about the development of energy cluster policies and initiatives. *First, there is a scarcity of research enhancing the design of place-based energy policies adjusted to various transition contexts* (Coenen & Truffer, 2012; Liu et al., 2020; Smith et al., 2004). A place-based approach means that individual national, industrial, and regional contexts become research topics on which broader policy ideas can be developed and implemented. Industrial transformation processes are the focus of public policies in international, national, regional, and local environments (Ashford et al., 2007; Chembessi et al., 2024; Coenen & Truffer, 2012; Schwabe, 2024). Energy clusters are placed in the local layer of these policies and can be a crucial instrument to build socioeconomic structures that initiate the green transition from the bottom up. Due to their small size, they represent niches for further replication and diffusion to larger territorial units (Bohatkiewicz-Czaicka & Gancarczyk, 2025). The opportunity of a bottom-up transition to green niches that can be further proliferated is especially relevant for Central and Eastern European economies, including Poland (Micek et al., 2021; Surwillo, 2022). These countries are characterized by energy-intensive industries that unfavorably affect the environment, requiring a major industrial transformation toward sustainability (Campos-Romero et al., 2024). Their policies aimed at energy clusters are currently in the early stages of development with respect to ecosystem governance structures and industrial transitions (Dragan, 2020; Elzen & Wieczorek, 2005; Grigore & Dragan, 2020; Mirowski & Kubica, 2016).

Second, a conceptual background for energy-focused SIT is needed and to identify the policy arrangements that favor or impede this transition (Micek et al., 2021; Surwillo, 2022). Energy-sustainable industrial transformation (ESIT) can be achieved through institutional solutions such as energy cluster initiatives (Ashford et al., 2007; Grigore & Dragan, 2020). The theoretical lens of institutions is suitable to highlight policy directions for industrial change in a complex territorial context (Benner, 2021). With a few exceptions

DOI: 10.4324/9781003623540-4

(Smith et al., 2004; Speck et al., 2023; Trejo-Nieto, 2021), the recognition of socioeconomic governance in industrial transformation is under-researched. In particular, cluster initiatives as a governance solution that improve the collaborations of various stakeholders to produce a local industrial path represent a policy tool that is underexploited in the context of Central and Eastern Europe, including Poland (Götz, 2021; Jasiński et al., 2021; Manowska et al., 2017; Mataczyńska & Kucharska, 2020; Meshkov, 2019; Mucha-Kuś et al., 2021; Surwillo, 2022; Tauron Polska Energia, 2024; Wiseman, 2023).

Third, the literature on energy clusters and policies is in the exploratory stage and predominantly includes qualitative case studies (Afeltowicz et al., 2024; Micek et al., 2021; Surwillo, 2022). This brings the value of in-depth exploration of particular phenomena and contexts and enables analytical generalizations. However, a synthesis and a statistical generalization are conducive to understanding the current state and setting up future research directions, which benefits science and practice (Meshkov, 2019). Therefore, we need larger samples of cases and observations to provide evidence from which stronger generalizations and policy recommendations can be derived.

The above knowledge gaps justify the research problem of how energy cluster policies can enhance sustainable industrial transformation set out in this monograph. Consequently, the objective of our empirical research is to identify the progress of the energy cluster policies and the development stages, drivers, and obstacles of local energy clusters. This main purpose will be implemented by addressing the following detailed objectives, namely, to i) identify the advancement of energy cluster policies in Poland considering a multiscalar context at the local, regional, country, and international levels, ii) identify the development phases and types of energy cluster initiatives in Poland, iii) identify the barriers and drivers of energy cluster initiatives in Poland, and iv) synthesize the recommendations for energy cluster policies to enhance sustainable industrial transformation. Related with these objectives are four research questions that this study is intended to address.

RQ1. What is the advancement of energy cluster policies in Poland considering a multiscalar context at the local, country, and international levels?
RQ2. What are the development phases of the energy cluster initiatives in Poland?
RQ3. What are the barriers and drivers of energy cluster initiatives in Poland?
RQ4. What are the recommendations for energy cluster policies to enhance sustainable industrial transformation?

The general argument of our research framework and the entire monograph (Figure 3.1) is that the advancement of policies for energy-sustainable industrial transformation through cluster initiatives can be identified and explained by acknowledging institutional arrangements, including local socioeconomic governance within cluster initiatives, as well as country and international law and policies.

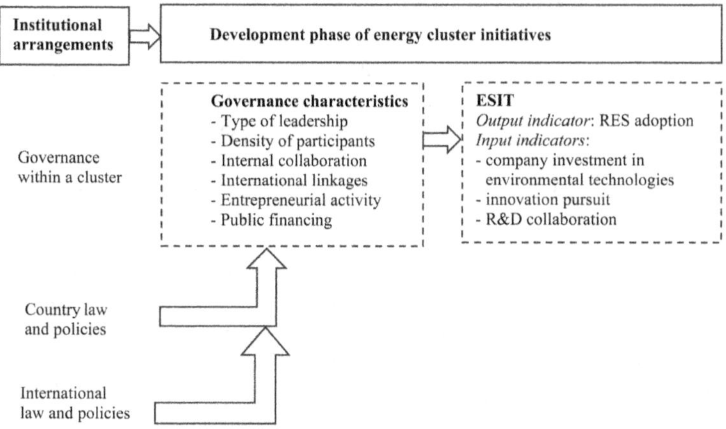

Figure 3.1 A research framework for evaluating the advancement of policies for ESIT through cluster initiatives

The research framework presents causal relationships between institutional arrangements and the advancement of policies for ESIT through cluster initiatives (Acemoglu et al., 2002; Benner, 2021; Gancarczyk et al., 2023; Williamson, 2000). ESIT is a type of sustainable industrial transformation focused on the energy industry. It represents a change in the structure of the energy industry, which addresses not only economic objectives but reconciles efficiency with environmental and social goals (Grillitsch, 2015; Hassink et al., 2019; Luken & Castellanos-Silveria, 2011; Oinas et al., 2018; Trejo-Nieto, 2021). In the context of energy clusters, it means that the cluster progresses toward the development of technology and innovation and renewable sources of energy.

The framework proposes that institutions are interacting and mutually affecting (Helmke & Levitsky, 2004; Williamson, 2000; Zukauskaite et al., 2017). Namely, institutional arrangements and at the country and international levels affect governance within a cluster at the local level. Cluster governance is a complex theoretical variable represented by a set of detailed variables. Institutions of governance represent an institutional structure that affects the functioning of a particular system, such as a cluster or territorial community (Williamson, 2000; Zukauskaite et al., 2017). Cluster governance encompasses internal rules of its functioning, such as the density of participation, type of leadership, internal collaboration, international linkages, entrepreneurial activity, and public financing (Brown & Mason, 2017; Colombelli et al., 2019; Gereffi & Lee, 2016). According to the existing literature, the cluster development phase is associated with the advancement of governance and ESIT (Brown & Mason, 2017; Colombelli et al., 2019; Gereffi & Lee, 2016).

ESIT, as an expected effect of energy cluster policies and its governance, can be approximated by the adoption of RES, as the output variable

(Deutz et al., 2024; Lowitzsch et al., 2020; Nadeem et al., 2023; Schwabe, 2024). Another dimension of ESIT is represented by input indicators of technology and innovation development, such as company investment in environmental technologies, innovation pursuit, and research and development (R&D) collaboration (Bohatkiewicz-Czaicka & Gancarczyk, 2025; Brown & Mason, 2017; Gancarczyk, 2019). In summary, the advance of energy cluster policies can be considered from the angle of the cluster development phase marked by the related characteristics of governance and ESIT. Furthermore, the framework assumes causal relationships between the institutional arrangements at the country and international levels, the cluster governance, and the ESIT (Acemoglu et al., 2002; Ostrom, 2010). Namely, the country and international institutional frameworks affect the institutions of governance within the cluster, with the latter resulting in different levels of ESIT. The theoretical constructs and relationships highlighted in Figure 3.1 of the research framework will be further tested empirically.

The framework follows the place-based logic that energy cluster policies and their respective initiatives are heterogeneous and the research should not seek one average or one size fits all solutions, but rather capture the existing variety as alternative profiles of local communities at different development phases (Broadhurst et al., 2021; O'Connor et al., 2017). Furthermore, the proposed framework avoids a static approach and assumes dynamic transitions of clusters among the identified profiles or development phases (Colombelli et al., 2019; Spigel, 2022). The transitions among the development stages described by the sets of variables also alleviate a reductionism approach when only individual and isolated factors are considered. Furthermore, alternative profiles assume an evolutionary approach, such as upgrading the existing cluster phase to more developed ones (De Marchi et al., 2018; Gereffi & Lee, 2016).

As a basis for empirical investigation, the framework can also be interpreted from the process perspective, as comprising three phases. In the first phase, the multiscalar institutional conditions should be described. In the second phase, the development stages or profiles of the energy clusters are identified. In the third phase, research questions regarding the characteristics and needs of clusters at various stages of development will be explored to derive policy recommendations.

3.2 Methods, Data Sources, and Research Procedure

Methods and Analytical Techniques

In the theoretical part of the monograph, we adopt the method of narrative literature review. The review covered theoretical literature and empirical studies in industrial policy, clusters and cluster evolution, regional industrial transformation, sustainable industrial transformation focused on energy, and institutional and coevolutionary approaches in economics.

Table 3.1 Methods and analytical techniques

Methods	*Analytical techniques*	*Sources of data and information*
Literature review	Narrative review of the literature Qualitative content analysis	Theoretical literature and empirical studies in industrial policy, clusters and cluster evolution, regional industrial transformation, energy-focused sustainable industrial transformation, as well as institutional and coevolutionary approaches in economics
Analysis of secondary sources	Qualitative content analysis	Reports, previous research on energy clusters, and evaluations of energy policy
Survey	Descriptive statistics, principal component analysis, taxonomical clustering analysis by k-means	Responses to survey questionnaires
Semi-structured interviews	Qualitative content analysis	Responses to semi-structured interviews, natural observation during telephone and online discussions

Source: own elaboration.

In the empirical part, to verify the research framework (Figure 3.1) *and to ensure a granular understanding of the empirical evidence, we used a mixed-method approach.* The latter included analysis of secondary sources and a survey method among Polish energy cluster initiatives enhanced by semi-structured interviews with the cluster administration. Given a large set of variables and a small N sample investigated, our analytical methods included descriptive statistics; exploratory data analysis, such as principal component analysis; and cluster taxonomical analysis. Aligned with the research framework, we used a taxonomical method of clustering by k-means to identify the configurations of the cluster characteristics, that is, unique profiles of their governance and ESIT (Jolliffe, 2002; Sanguansat, 2012). Consequently, based on the quantitative taxonomical approach, energy clusters can be categorized into development phases (Breslin & Gatrell, 2020). Furthermore, a qualitative content analysis of the insights from the interviews and a secondary data analysis of reports, previous research on energy clusters and evaluations of energy policy were conducted (Boje & Rosile, 2020). Table 3.1 presents the methods, related analytical techniques, as well as the sources of data and information used in our study.

Data Sources

The main empirical evidence stemmed from one country setting of Poland; however, this context of energy cluster policies will further be investigated and discussed against the related international experience of other European countries and beyond (Hassink, 2019; Mucha-Kuś et al., 2021b; Smith et al., 2004). The choice of the Polish sample of energy cluster initiatives and the context of one country was justified by several arguments.

First, focusing on one country ensures a homogeneous economic and legal system to understand the conditions for energy cluster policies (Acemoglu et al., 2002; Hodgson, 2015; North, 2010). At the same time, as a European Union (EU) member, Poland can exemplify the multiscalar institutional context stemming from the economic integration and hence the influence of international laws and policies (Benner, 2021; Bessagnet et al., 2021; Chen & Hassink, 2020). Poland is required to comply with regulations from the EU, as well as international agreements and commitments made to environmental protection organizations, such as the United Nations Framework Convention on Climate Change (UNFCCC), the Kyoto Protocol, the Paris Agreement, the Convention on Biological Diversity (CBD), the Aarhus Convention, the Stockholm Convention on Persistent Organic Pollutants, and the 2030 National Environmental Policy (PEP2030). The focus on Polish energy clusters is valuable, since Poland represents a country experienced in systemic transitions, and, being a part of the EU, it integrates national policies with the EU strategies (Campos-Romero et al., 2024). In this vein, our research results will provide values and recommendations relevant beyond national boundaries.

Second, the Polish context of sustainable energy transitions is challenging (Dragan, 2020; Micek et al., 2021; Surwillo, 2022). Public policies, including energy cluster initiatives, are therefore crucial for industrial transformation processes and require scientific focus. Energy-intensive industries and a small share of renewable sources in our country are accompanied by a reluctance to transition costs and moderate public recognition of green transformation (Campos-Romero et al., 2024; Grigore & Dragan, 2020).

The policies oriented toward local energy clusters are at the initial stages in terms of ecosystemic governance structures and industrial technological transitions (Dragan, 2020; Grigore & Dragan, 2020; Mucha-Kuś et al., 2021). Consequently, transition costs are perceived as high by society (Sołtysik & Kozakiewicz, 2018; Szewranski et al., 2019). Energy cluster initiatives, cooperatives, and communities face economic and legal barriers, with a predominant attitude to rely on cooperation agreements and remain alert for public financing opportunities rather than actively operate (Jasiński et al., 2021; Surwillo, 2022). These policy initiatives suffer from infrastructure, capital, and management shortages, as well as limited social trust (Dragan, 2020; Micek et al., 2021; Surwillo, 2022; Wawrzyniak et al., 2021). The current assessment of the energy cluster population points to 130–140 initiatives formalized and around 50 units actively operating, while public policy programmatic documents aim at 300 units by 2030 (Gryszczuk, 2024; Ministry of Climate and Environment, 2021). However, a considerable proportion of the formal entities reported have been inactive, waiting for the improved economic and legal environment.

Third, the place-based approach to industrial transformation is promoted in the New Industrial Policy (NIP), including the turn of renewable energy. This requires evidence-based research in various transition contexts (Coenen & Truffer, 2012; Liu, 2020; Luken & Castellanos-Silveria, 2011; Smith et al., 2004). NIP has gained prominence both in the EU and worldwide (Chen & Hassink, 2020; Ministry of Climate and Environment, 2021). This policy acknowledges the place-based approach to designing and implementing territorial and industrial strategies. Our study concentrates on an underresearched local level of industrial transition in a challenging context (Afeltowicz et al., 2024; Broadhurst et al., 2021; Dreyfus & Suwa, 2022; Gancarczyk et al., 2024).

Fourth, this research will clearly define the scope of generalization (Benner, 2021; Breslin & Gatrell, 2020). Our analysis will be specifically related to energy cluster policies, highlighting their characteristics within the European and international contexts (Mucha-Kuś et al., 2021; Smith et al., 2004). This approach allows us to acknowledge the diversity of these clusters while also identifying shared institutional and economic characteristics that transcend national boundaries.

We used primary and secondary sources of data. Primary data were drawn from the survey among Polish energy cluster initiatives and semi-structured interviews. The engagement was established with two major associations of energy cluster initiatives, namely the National Chamber of Energy Clusters (NCEC), which officially records 93 initiatives, and the Cluster Coordinator (CC), representing 63 entities led by local governments. The survey was administered in two rounds, separately among the NCEC and CC communities. This was due to different central tenants in these initiatives, companies or local governments, which required establishing a unique involvement with key respondents and experts, as well as a verification of the relevance and face validity of the research tool (Wright et al., 2020).

As an introductory data collection and to understand the research field, eight semi-structured interviews were conducted by two researchers using the telephone and an online communicator with a manager and a staff member (Saris & Gallhofer, 2014; Simsek & Veiga, 2000, 2001). The interviews included questions about the legal framework for cluster initiatives, the structure of their association, and the level of member responsiveness to assess the prospects for collecting empirical evidence (Boje & Rosile, 2020). The notes from the observations were discussed, and the conclusions were agreed by the two researchers involved, contributing to the development of a survey tool, that is, a questionnaire form. The research tool was ultimately verified through face validation by two NCEC leaders and one administration staff, and through a pilot study among three cluster initiatives. This feedback helped to refine the questions and resulted in modifications that improved the accuracy and relevancy of the questions. The NCEC administration provided a database with email contacts to the associated 93 energy cluster entities. Additionally, the distribution of the survey was supported by a cover letter from two leaders of this association, emphasizing the importance of the survey for their practice and policy.

This first-round survey was distributed online, with the anonymity of the respondents ensured and duration from November to December 2023. Expectedly, this action raised a small response rate. To address this problem, one of the researchers addressed all entities recorded in the NCEC database by phone. These semi-structured and concise interviews were aimed at highlighting the objectives of the research and thus convincing the addressee to participate in the survey, as well as learning about their perceived drivers and obstacles in developing local energy communities (Wright et al., 2020). The important result of these telephone interviews was recognition of the fraction of energy cluster initiatives that are actively operating and the determination of the proportion that should be treated as inactive. Based on telephone feedback and the identification of non-valid contact details, it was determined that approximately 46 cluster initiatives should be regarded as active, while 47 were found to be inactive, representing about 50% of the official database. Telephone queries resulted in the final sample of 24 complete questionnaires, forming 52% of 46 active entities. The reported response rate corresponded to the experience revealed by NCEC staff.

The second round of interviews was directed to members of another association of energy cluster initiatives, namely the CC group, which gathers entities led by local governments. The procedure of establishing engagement with the CC board members and getting their face validation of the research tool was similar as in the case of the first-round survey. Two researchers conducted four telephone orientation interviews with one member of the CC board. The board members confirmed the validity of the questionnaire without introducing any changes. The online survey was administered from December 2023 to March 2024, targeting 63 officially registered entities, with the anonymity of the respondents ensured. Due to the limited response rate, follow-up telephone contacts were conducted to check the proportion of active versus inactive entities.

These contacts also included short semi-structured interviews to provide orientation on the purpose of the study and gain insight into the conditions of operation of the clusters, including their barriers and drivers. In addition to the qualitative material transformed into research notes, this feedback revealed 25 active cases (around 40% of those officially registered) and 38 inactive cases, forming nearly 60% of the initial records. Recognizing the status of the central tenants in these initiatives, being local governments obliged to respond through a public information system, we also used this system to increase the response rate. The telephone contacts and the additional online distribution via the system of public administration raised 19 responses; that is, 80% of the CC associates identified as active. The accuracy of this assessment of the response rate is in accordance with the observations of the CC leader who shared concerns about the reluctance of his members to interact and provide feedback.

As a final sample, the two-round survey process produced 43 complete responses, giving a 60% share of the energy cluster initiatives actively operating in the NCEC and CC associations. However, according to recent assessments by the NCEC leader, the group of active energy clusters in Poland amounts to around 50 entities, which would increase the representatives of the sample to 86% of the operating clusters (Gryszczuk, 2024). The two researchers involved discussed and agreed on additional interview material from the notes from the semi-structured interviews. The notes were taken, including the talks of the respondents and their own observations, amounting to 30 normalized pages. The review of key secondary sources of reports, evaluations, and academic books and papers related to the phenomenon of Polish energy clusters produced material of approximately 2,000 normalized pages.

Research Procedure

The research procedure included the following interrelated steps:

- literature review to identify research gaps in the area of energy cluster policies towards sustainable industrial transformation;
- based on the identified research gaps, formulating the research problem, the main aim and detailed objectives of the research;
- formulating research questions corresponding with research gaps, the problem identified, as well as the aim of the study;
- determining the scope and empirical base of the research;
- determining the methods, analytical techniques, and sources of data and information;
- identifying the research sample and engaging with the key research stakeholders;
- development of the research tool and refinement through face validation with key stakeholders and a pilot study;
- data collection, recording, and organizing;
- operationalization of the main research variables included in the research framework;
- data evaluation, processing, and interpretation;
- systemizing the findings; and
- synthesis of research and formulation of conclusions and recommendations for research and practice.

3.3 Operationalization and Measurement of the Research Framework Variables

Operationalization of the Research Framework Variables

Guided by the research framework (Figure 3.1), where the theoretical variables and their relationships were highlighted, as well as the theoretical considerations in Chapters 1 and 2, we designed a questionnaire that reflected the operationalization and measurement of the respective theoretical conditions (institutional arrangements at the international, country, and local cluster governance levels) for ESIT (O'Kane et al., 2021; Simsek & Veiga, 2000). The theoretical variables required the operationalization to the observed variables in terms of facts, perceptions, and behaviors of the organizations studied. Table 3.2 presents the operationalization of the variables of the research framework, namely, their meaning and conceptual foundations, the source literature, and the relationship with appropriate research questions.

We assume that the governance indicators act as stimulants for ESIT and when the values of governance and ESIT indicators increase, the cluster development stage is upgraded (De Marchi & Alford, 2022; Gancarczyk & Bohatkiewicz, 2018; Gereffi & Lee, 2016). The cluster governance concept is rooted in New Institutional Economics, coevolutionary approach, and cluster concept, including coevolutionary and life cycle approach to industrial agglomerations (Martin & Sunley, 2017; Ostrom, 2010; Williamson, 2000). Cluster governance represents an institutional structure that affects its functioning; internal sets of rules and norms such as the density of participation, internal collaboration, international linkages, entrepreneurial activity, and public financing (Brown & Mason, 2017; Colombelli et al., 2019; Gereffi & Lee, 2016; Helmke & Levitsky, 2004; Markusen, 1996; Williamson, 2000; Zukauskaite et al., 2017).

The governance indicators include cluster leadership (GLEAD), a complex variable of the density of participation, which embraces the overall number of cluster participants (GDON), number of companies (GDCN), and number of R&D entities (GDRN) (Gancarczyk, 2019; Gancarczyk & Konopa, 2021). Moreover it encompasses a complex variable of cluster collaboration with local government (GCLG), among companies (GCC), between companies and R&D entities (GCRD), and a level of formalization of collaboration among companies (GCCF) (Apa et al., 2021; Broadhurst et al., 2021). Furthermore, cluster governance is featured by linkages with international environment, in particular, international knowledge transfer collaboration (GINT) (Bai et al., 2021). Entrepreneurial activity approximated by the number of startups in a cluster (GSTR) and public financing (GPF) complete the features of governance characteristics derived from theoretical considerations in Chapter 1.

We will also explore the cluster development stage from the angle of ESIT, including both the adoption of renewable energy sources (RESs)

Table 3.2 Operationalization of the research framework variables

Variable	*Conceptual foundations and meaning*	*Source literature*	*Relationship with research questions*
Energy-sustainable industrial transformation (ESIT)	The concept of regional industrial transformation developed towards sustainability in the energy industry; the variable comprising the cluster progress towards renewable energy sources, such as the adoption of RES, and technological and innovation development towards ESIT (company investment in environmental technologies, innovation, R&D collaboration).	(Chembessi et al., 2024; Grillitsch, 2015; Hassink et al., 2019; Luken & Castellanos-Silveria, 2011; Oinas et al., 2018; Schwabe, 2024; Trejo-Nieto, 2021)	*RQ1.* What is the advancement of energy cluster policies in Poland considering a multiscalar context at the local, country, and international levels? *RQ2.* What are the development phases of energy cluster initiatives in Poland? *RQ3.* What are the barriers and drivers of energy cluster initiatives in Poland? *RQ4.* What are the recommendations for energy cluster policies to enhance sustainable industrial transformation?
Cluster governance	New Institutional Economics, coevolutionary approach, cluster concept, cluster evolution (life cycle). Cluster governance represents an institutional structure that affects its functioning; internal sets of rules and norms such as the density of participation, internal collaboration, international linkages, entrepreneurial activity, and public financing.	(Brown & Mason, 2017; Colombelli et al., 2019; Gereffi & Lee, 2016; Helmke & Levitsky, 2004; Markusen, 1996; Williamson, 2000; Zukauskaite et al., 2017)	*RQ1.* What is the advancement of energy cluster policies in Poland considering a multiscalar context at the local, country, and international levels? *RQ2.* What are the development phases of energy cluster initiatives in Poland?
Cluster development phase according to governance and ESIT progress	Coevolutionary approach, cluster evolution (life cycle). Cluster development phases include birth, intermediate, and advanced stages, as marked by level of density, collaboration, entrepreneurial activity and public financing.		*RQ2.* What are the development phases of energy cluster initiatives in Poland? *RQ3.* What are the barriers and drivers of energy cluster initiatives in Poland?

(*Continued*)

Table 3.2 (Continued)

Variable	*Conceptual foundations and meaning*	*Source literature*	*Relationship with research questions*
Institutional arrangements at the international level	New Institutional Economics. Legal and policy-related institutions.	(Acemoglu et al., 2002; Colombelli et al., 2019; Gereffi & Lee, 2016; Helmke & Levitsky, 2004; North, 2010; Ostrom, 2010; Williamson, 2000; Zukauskaite et al., 2017)	*RQ1.* What is the advancement of energy cluster policies in Poland considering a multiscalar context at the local, country, and international levels? *RQ3.* What are the barriers and drivers of energy cluster initiatives in Poland? *RQ4.* What are the recommendations for energy cluster policies to enhance sustainable industrial transformation (SIT)?
Institutional arrangements at the country level	New Institutional Economics, legal and policy-related institutions.		*RQ1.* What is the advancement of energy cluster policies in Poland considering a multiscalar context at the local, country, and international levels? *RQ3.* What are the barriers and drivers of energy cluster initiatives in Poland? *RQ4.* What are the recommendations for energy cluster policies to enhance sustainable industrial transformation (SIT)?

Source: own elaboration.

(ESITRES), and input indicators of industrial transitions that reflect technological and innovation advances. ESIT represents the concept of regional industrial transformation theoretically expanded towards sustainability in the energy industry (Chembessi et al., 2024; Oinas et al., 2018; Schwabe, 2024; Trejo-Nieto, 2021). According to the theoretical analysis in Chapter 1, these inputs to ESIT cover company investment in environmental technologies (ESITEN), innovation pursuit (ESITRIN), and collaboration with research entities (ESITRD). The variants of the development phases will be identified according to the configurations of cluster governance and ESIT characteristics. This, in turn, allows for profiling the cluster advancement and related policies.

Following the assumptions of an institutional approach, we will investigate legal and policy-related institutions at the country and international levels to understand their influence on cluster governance (Acemoglu et al., 2002; Gereffi & Lee, 2016; North, 2010; Ostrom, 2010; Williamson, 2000).

Measurement of Variables

Table 3.3 presents the measurement of the observed variables and the corresponding sources of information and data. In addition to the variables directly related to the research framework, the survey questionnaire included other characteristics of the groups of entities. These cluster attributes refer to their resource potential, such as installed energy power, territorial scope and population covered, and capability potential, including year of establishment to reflect age and experience gained and areas of activity. These properties are indicated in Table 3.3 according to their measurement approach.

Based on the research findings, Tables 3.4 and 3.5 present the scale reliability for the constructs of cluster governance (G) and cluster energy-sustainable industrial transformation (ESIT). Due to the different scales of items, the data was standardized prior to performing the analysis.

The cluster governance scale (Table 3.4) meets the reliability criteria of the scale according to Cronbach's alpha, since the value of 0.880 is at the appropriate level to acknowledge the consistency of the scale. This was achieved after removing the item of public financing (GPF), which proved to be negatively correlated with other items. Although removing the proxy of entrepreneurial activity (GSTR) would slightly increase the value of alpha, it would more considerably worsen the inter-item correlation, bringing it at the edge of the accepted value of 0.50. The current value of 0.444 shows that the scale reflects different dimensions of the phenomenon studied and enriches the possibility of interpretation. The following Table 3.5 presents the scale reliability for cluster ESIT.

Table 3.3 Measurement of the research framework variables

Theoretical variable	*Observed variable name and code*	*Data or information source*	*Measurement*
Energy-sustainable industrial transformation (ESIT)	*Output indicator*: the share of RES in the overall energy production of an energy cluster (ESITRES) *Input indicators*: • Energy cluster companies investment in environmental technologies (ESITEN) • Energy cluster innovation pursuit (ESITIN) • Cluster collaboration with R&D entities (universities, research institutes, academic enterprises, specialized R&D enterprises) (ESITRD)	Own survey data, analysis of secondary sources	*Output indicator:* percentage of RES in the total energy production; 0%–20% – 0; 21% or more – 1 *Input indicators*: • Cluster companies investment in environmental technologies – 1, lack of investment – 0 • Innovation activities pursued – 1, lack of innovation activities – 0 • Energy cluster collaboration with any of respective R&D entities – 1, lack of R&D collaboration – 0
Cluster governance (G)	Cluster leadership by local government or companies (GLEAD)	Own survey data, analysis of secondary sources	Company-led cluster – 1, local government-led cluster – 0,
	Density of participation • Overall number of cluster participants (GDON) • Number of companies (GDCN) • Number of R&D entities (GDRN)		Density of participation (Likert 1–5 according to participant numbers in each category)
	Internal collaboration with local government (GCLG), between companies (GCC), between companies and R&D entities (GCRD)		Internal collaboration (intensity of collaboration reported on the Likert scale 1–5)
	Level of formalization of the collaboration among companies (GCCF)		Likert scale 1–5 (informal collaboration – 1, formal agreements – 2, joint investment 3, joint ventures – 4, company integration – 5)
	International knowledge transfer collaboration (GINT)		International collaboration (intensity of collaboration reported on the Likert scale 1–5)
	Entrepreneurial activity as a number of startups in a cluster (GSTR)		Likert 1–5 according to the number of startups
	Public financing (GPF)		Likert 1–3, no financing sources or public financing present as one source – 1, public financing present as one of the sources – 2, other than public financing – 3

(Continued)

Table 3.3 (Continued)

Theoretical variable	*Observed variable name and code*	*Data or information source*	*Measurement*
Cluster development phase according to governance and ESIT advancement	The levels of the above observed variables for the governance and ESIT theoretical variables will denote the cluster development phase. The progressive dynamics will be as follows: from low to increasing internal collaboration, from low to increasing international collaboration, from low to increasing entrepreneurial activity, from high to decreasing public financing	Own survey data, analysis of secondary sources, semi-structured interviews	The energy clusters classified according to the development phase by means of k-means clustering
Institutional arrangements at the international and country levels	Laws and policies regarding energy cluster initiatives, energy communities, and energy cooperatives	Own survey, analysis of secondary sources, semi-structured interviews	The survey respondents were asked to select the major economic resource constraints they face (nominal scale with types of constraints), evaluate the quality of legislatures on energy clusters (1–5 Likert scale), and provide open-response recommendations to improve the economic and legal environment for energy clusters
Cluster resource potential	Installed energy power (IEP)	Own survey, analysis of secondary sources	<5 megawatt 5–50 megawatt >50 megawatt
	Territorial scope (TER)		1–3 communes – 1 4–5 communes – 2 1 county – 3
	Population covered (POP)		<20,000 inhabitants – 1, 20,000–50,000 inhabitants – 2 50,000–100,000 inhabitants – 3 >100,000 – 4
Cluster capability potential	Year of establishment (the proxy for cluster age and experience and hence capability potential) (AGE)	Own survey, analysis of secondary sources	2021–2023 – 0 2016–2018 – 1
	Area of activity (ACT)		Nominal scale with areas of activity; one activity – 1, two activities – 2, at least three activities – 3

Source: own elaboration.

Table 3.4 Scale reliability for the construct of cluster governance

	Summary for scale: mean = –0.000; std. dv. = 6.934; valid N: 43; Cronbach's alpha: 0.880; standardized alpha: 0.841; average inter-item corr.: 0.444				
Variables covering G	*Mean if deleted**	*Variannce if deleted*	*Std. dv. if deleted*	*Item-total correl.*	*Alpha if deleted*
GLEAD	–0.000	38.813	6.230	0.583	0.870
GDON	–0.000	37.743	6.144	0.679	0.863
GDCN	–0.000	37.618	6.133	0.690	0.862
GDRN	–0.000	38.528	6.207	0.608	0.868
GCLG	–0.000	37.266	6.105	0.723	0.860
GCC	–0.000	37.359	6.112	0.714	0.860
GCCF	–0.000	38.945	6.241	0.571	0.871
GCRD	–0.000	37.99131	6.164	0.656	0.865
GINT	–0.000	39.07000	6.251	0.560	0.872
GSTR	–0.000	42.14994	6.492	0.299	0.890

Note: * – after data standardization.
Source: own research.

As demonstrated in Table 3.5, the scale for cluster governance meets the threshold of reliability according to Cronbach's alpha exceeding 0.70. An inter-item correlation of 0.392 confirms that the scale captures well a variety of the construct dimensions. Although deletion of ESITRES could have increased the alpha value, we checked that inter-item correlation would have crossed the level of 0.50, meaning the items are repetitive.

Table 3.5 Scale reliability for the construct of cluster energy-sustainable industrial transformation

	Summary for scale: mean = –0.000; std. dv. = 2.904; valid N: 43; Cronbach's alpha: 0.701; standardized alpha: 0.701; average inter-item corr.: 0.392				
Variables covering ESIT	*Mean if deleted**	*Var. if deleted*	*Std. dv. if deleted*	*Item-total correl.*	*Alpha if deleted*
ESITRES	–0.000	5.984	2.446	0.263	0.765
ESITEN	–0.000	5.046	2.246	0.498	0.629
ESITIN	–0.000	4.470	2.114	0.667	0.517
ESITRD	–0.000	4.875	2.208	0.546	0.598

Note: * – after data standardization.
Source: own research.

3.4 Characteristics of the Research Sample

Table 3.6 presents the characteristics of the research sample of Polish energy clusters, according to the control variables classified into resource potential and capability potential. It also highlights how these attributes are associated with leadership type (GLEAD) and adoption of RES (ESITRES). The relationships between the characteristics of the resource and capability referred and the adoption of RES were investigated to highlight the potential influence of these attributes on the main output measure of the dependent variable of ESIT (Chembessi et al., 2024b). Due to a different leadership type, it is also

Table 3.6 Polish energy clusters resource and capability potential – a research sample characteristics

Characteristics		*N*	*Chi square; Cramer's V; Spearman rank R for ESITRES*	*Chi square; Cramer's V; Spearman rank R for GLEAD*
Cluster resource potential	Installed energy power (IEP) <5 megawatt 5–50 megawatt >50 megawatt	29 10 4	8.155*, df = 2; 0.436*; 0.427**	6.777*, df = 2; 0.397*; 0.361**
	Territorial scope (TER) 1–3 communes 4–5 communes 1 county	16 14 13	3.475, df = 2; 0.284; 0.250	10.049*, df = 2; 0.483*; –0.090
	Population covered (POP) <20,000 20,000–50,000 50,000–100,000 >100,000	8 12 12 11	0.863, df = 3; 0.142; 0.138	5.109, df = 3; 0.345; 0.334*
Cluster capability potential	Year of establishment (AGE) 2016–2018 2021–2023	21 22	7.308*, df = 1; 0.412*; 0.412*	19.996*, df = 1; 0.563*; 0.682*
	Areas of activity (ACT) 1 area 2 areas 3 or more areas	22 15 6	0.117, df = 2; 0.521; –0.051	7.920**, df = 2; 0.483**; 0.060
RES adoption	Share of RES (ESITRES) 0%–20% 21%–100%	34 9	N/A	5.049**, df = 1; 0.343; 0.343**
Leadership type	Leadership (GLEAD) Local government Companies	19 24	5.049**, df = 1; 0.343; 0.343**	N/A

Notes: N = 43; * – $p < 0.05$; ** – $p < 0.01$.

Source: own research.

useful for decision makers to understand the implications of the central tenant being either public administration authorities or companies (Broadhurst et al., 2021; Debizet et al., 2022; Dreyfus & Suwa, 2022; Gancarczyk et al., 2024).

The resource potential of the energy clusters investigated was considered from the angle of installed energy power, territorial scope, and population covered. These aspects of resources are limited to the local reach by the legal definition of energy initiatives, and the smallest units in terms of these resource criteria predominate. However, the sample varies within these defined local boundaries. In terms of installed energy power, the clusters predominantly govern below 5 megawatts (29 subjects), while the ranges from 5 to 50 megawatts and more than 50 megawatts are less popular (10 and 4 subjects, accordingly). The local territorial administration system in Poland includes the communes as the smallest administrative unit. County boundaries comprise sets of communes, which are middle-level administration between the communes and regions, the latter being the largest units. The limited territorial scope of 1 to 3 communes is represented by 16 clusters, while 14 initiatives cover 4 to 5 communes, and 13 of them operate in one county. The density of population covered by the administrative units can differ, so it is informative to understand the distribution of inhabitants linked to the initiatives. Taking into account this aspect, 12 subjects are related to a population of 20,000 to 50,000 and 12 subjects to a population of 50,000 to 100,000. Eleven clusters cover the population of more than 100,000, and eight of them represent the community of less than 20,000 inhabitants.

Regarding the main reference variable for the above characteristics, the adoption of RES (ESITRES) of at least 21% in overall energy production was found in only nine initiatives. Eight of these cases were led by companies, while one case belongs to the group of local government-led initiatives. At the same time, 34 entities demonstrated RES below the 21% threshold. Similarly, the statistical tests in Table 3.6 reveal a significant and moderately positive relationship between the leadership of the firm in the groups and the adoption of RES by these entities.

The statistical test of the chi square, Cramer's V, and Spearman's rank R (Table 3.6) reveal the association between installed energy power and RES adoption; that is, the higher installed power is positively related to the achievement of ESITRES. Respective independence and correlation tests have also revealed a statistically significant and positive relation between installed power and the type of cluster leadership. The higher installed power is more typical of company-led clusters than of initiatives led by local governments.

The tests have not shown any statistically significant association between the territorial scope of the cluster activities and the adoption of RES. However, we observe a moderately positive and statistically significant relationship between territorial reach and leadership type, with company-led entities responsible for larger territories. The tests did not show statistically significant interdependencies between the number of population linked to the cluster and its adoption of

RES. However, a moderate and positive statistically significant correlation was confirmed between the larger population and the leadership of the cluster by the firms.

The capability potential of the sampled energy clusters was considered from the perspective of the year of establishment and areas of activity. The year of establishment and the related age of the unit imply its accumulated experience and competence. The analysis of this aspect revealed that there were two waves of cluster formation, namely 2016–2018 (21 subjects) and 2021–2023 (22 subjects), and the cohorts of the establishments are almost equal. Consequently, the records of operation of the initiatives do not exceed eight years. The main activities of the clusters include electricity production, distribution, and trade (37 clusters). Fourteen clusters provide energy storage and balance, and only seven of them are involved in the production and distribution of steam heat. The scope of these activities, in terms of the number of activities in the cluster portfolio, denotes the range of competences. From this angle, 17 groups focus on only one activity, 12 groups perform two activities, and 5 groups exercise at least three activities.

The statistical test of the chi square, Cramer's V, and Spearman's rank R (Table 3.6) reveal a moderately positive association between the previous year of establishment, and therefore a longer history of operations, and the adoption of RES. The relationship between operation history and leadership type is positive and significant, indicating that company-led clusters have a longer record of operation experience. The independence and correlation tests have not confirmed any dependence between the number of activities performed and ESITRES. However, they showed a moderately positive and significant relation between the type of leadership and the scope of activities, with a broader set of activities carried out by groups with firm leaders.

References

Acemoglu, D., Johnson, S., & Robinson, J. A. (2002). Reversal of fortune: Geography and institutions in the making of the modern world income distribution. *The Quarterly Journal of Economics, 117*(4), 1231–1294.

Afeltowicz, Ł., Nawojczyk, M., & Tyrała, R. (2024). Entrepreneurial actions in energy transition: A study of three local energy clusters in Poland. *European Urban and Regional Studies, 31*(2), 132–148. https://doi.org/10.1177/09697764231179667

Apa, R., De Marchi, V., Grandinetti, R., & Sedita, S. R. (2021). University-SME collaboration and innovation performance: The role of informal relationships and absorptive capacity. *The Journal of Technology Transfer, 46*, 961–988.

Ashford, N. A., Hafkamp, W., Prakke, F., & Vergragt, P. (2002). *Pathways to Sustainable Industrial Transformations: Co-optimising Competitiveness, Employment, and Environment.* In *Conference engineering education in sustainable development* (pp. 582–601). https://research.tudelft.nl/en/publications/pathways-to-sustainable-industrial-transformations-co-optimising-. Accessed December 28, 2024.

Bai, W., Johanson, M., Oliveira, L., & Ratajczak-Mrozek, M. (2021). The role of business and social networks in the effectual internationalization: Insights from emerging market SMEs. *Journal of Business Research, 129*, 96–109.

Benner, M. (2021). Retheorizing industrial–institutional coevolution: A multidimensional perspective. *Regional Studies*, 1–14.

Bessagnet, A., Crespo, J., & Vicente, J. (2021). Unraveling the multi-scalar and evolutionary forces of entrepreneurial ecosystems: A historical event analysis applied to IoT Valley. *Technovation, 108*, 102329. https://doi.org/10.1016/j.technovation.2021.102329

Bohatkiewicz-Czaicka, J., & Gancarczyk, M. (2025). *Industrial clusters in international value chains: Conceptual advancement and empirical evidence from European ICT clusters*. Taylor & Francis.

Boje, D., & Rosile, G. A. (2020). *How to use conversational storytelling interviews for your dissertation*. Edward Elgar Publishing.

Breslin, D., & Gatrell, C. (2020). Theorizing through literature reviews: The miner-prospector continuum. *Organizational Research Methods, 26*(1), 139–167. https://doi.org/10.1177/1094428120943288.

Broadhurst, K., Ferreira, J., & Berkeley, N. (2021). Collaborative leadership and place-based development. *Local Economy, 36*(2), 149–163.

Brown, R., & Mason, C. (2017). Looking inside the spiky bits: A critical review and conceptualisation of entrepreneurial ecosystems. *Small Business Economics, 49*(1), 11–30.

Campos-Romero, H., Rodil-Marzábal, Ó., & Gómez Pérez, A. L. (2024). Environmental asymmetries in global value chains: The case of the European automotive sector. *Journal of Cleaner Production, 449*, 141606. https://doi.org/10.1016/j.jclepro.2024.141606

Chembessi, C., Bourdin, S., & Torre, A. (2024). Towards a territorialisation of the circular economy: The proximity of stakeholders and resources matters. *Cambridge Journal of Regions, Economy and Society, 17*(3), rsae007.

Chen, Y., & Hassink, R. (2020). Multi-scalar knowledge bases for new regional industrial path development: Toward a typology. *European Planning Studies, 28*(12), 2489–2507. https://doi.org/10.1080/09654313.2020.1724265

Coenen, L., & Truffer, B. (2012). Places and spaces of sustainability transitions: Geographical contributions to an emerging research and policy field. *European Planning Studies, 20*(3), 367–374.

Colombelli, A., Paolucci, E., & Ughetto, E. (2019). Hierarchical and relational governance and the life cycle of entrepreneurial ecosystems. *Small Business Economics, 52*, 505–521.

Debizet, G., Pappalardo, M., & Wurtz, F. (2022). *Local energy communities: Emergence, places, organizations, decision tools*. Taylor & Francis.

De Marchi, V., & Alford, M. (2022). State policies and upgrading in global value chains: A systematic literature review. *Journal of International Business Policy, 5*(1), 88–111.

De Marchi, V., Giuliani, E., & Rabellotti, R. (2018). Do global value chains offer developing countries learning and innovation opportunities? *The European Journal of Development Research, 30*(3), 389–407.

Deutz, P., Jonas, A. E., Newsholme, A., Pusz, M., Rogers, H. A., Affolderbach, J., Baumgartner, R. J., & Ramos, T. B. (2024). The role of place in the development of a circular economy: a critical analysis of potential for social redistribution in Hull, UK. *Cambridge Journal of Regions, Economy and Society*, *17*(3), 551–564.

Dragan, D. (2020). Legal barriers to the development of energy clusters in Poland. *European Energy and Environmental Law Review*, *29*(1), 14–20.

Dreyfus, M., & Suwa, A. (2022). *Local energy governance: Opportunities and challenges for renewable and decentralised energy in France and Japan*. Routledge.

Elzen, B., & Wieczorek, A. (2005). Transitions towards sustainability through system innovation. *Technological Forecasting and Social Change*, *72*(6), 651–661.

Gancarczyk, M. (2019). The performance of high-growers and regional entrepreneurial ecosystems: A research framework. *Entrepreneurial Business and Economics Review*, *7*(3), 99–123. https://doi.org/10.15678/EBER.2019.070306

Gancarczyk, M., & Bohatkiewicz, J. (2018). Research streams in cluster upgrading. A literature review. *Journal of Entrepreneurship, Management and Innovation*, *14*(4), 17–42.

Gancarczyk, M., Gancarczyk, J., & Reichel, M. (2024). Revitalizing forgotten spaces through local leadership and social entrepreneurial ecosystems: The case of Muszyna commune. In M. del Carmen Sánchez-Carreira, P. J. R. Mourão, & B. Blanco-Varela (Eds.), *European regional policy and development* (pp. 105–134). Routledge.

Gancarczyk, M., & Konopa, S. (2021). Exploring the governance of entrepreneurial ecosystems for productive high growth. *Foresight and STI Governance*, *15*(4), 9–21. https://doi.org/10.17323/2500-2597.2021.4.9.21

Gancarczyk, M., Najda-Janoszka, M., Gancarczyk, J., & Hassink, R. (2023). Exploring regional innovation policies and regional industrial transformation from a coevolutionary perspective: The case of Małopolska, Poland. *Economic Geography*, *99*(1), 51–80. https://doi.org/10.1080/00130095.2022.2120465

Gereffi, G., & Lee, J. (2016). Economic and social upgrading in global value chains and industrial clusters: Why governance matters. *Journal of Business Ethics*, *133*(1), 25–38.

Götz, M. (2021). *Clusters, digital transformation and regional development in Germany*. Routledge.

Grigore, A. M., & Dragan, I. M. (2020). Towards sustainable entrepreneurial ecosystems in a transitional economy: An analysis of two Romanian city-regions through the lens of entrepreneurs. *Sustainability (Switzerland)*, *12*(15). https://doi.org/10.3390/su12156061

Grillitsch, M. (2015). Institutional layers, connectedness and change: Implications for economic evolution in regions. *European Planning Studies*, *23*(10), 2099–2124.

Gryszczuk, A. (2024, January 15). *Zmiany w prawie dla klastrów energii. Czego zabrakło? (Changes in the law for energy clusters. What is missing?)* [Interview]. https://www.gramwzielone.pl/trendy/20178467/zmiany-w-prawie-dla-klastrow-energii-czego-zabraklo

Hassink, R. (2019). How to decontextualize in economic geography? *Dialogues in Human Geography*, *9*(3), 279–282.

Hassink, R., Isaksen, A., & Trippl, M. (2019). Towards a comprehensive understanding of new regional industrial path development. *Regional Studies*, *53*(11), 1636–1645. https://doi.org/10.1080/00343404.2019.1566704

Helmke, G., & Levitsky, S. (2004). Informal institutions and comparative politics: A research agenda. *Perspectives on Politics*, *2*(4), 725–740.

Hodgson, G. M. (2015). On defining institutions: Rules versus equilibria. *Journal of Institutional Economics*, *11*(3), 497–505.

Jasiński, J., Kozakiewicz, M., & Sołtysik, M. (2021). Determinants of energy cooperatives' development in rural areas—Evidence from Poland. *Energies*, *14*(2), 319. https://doi.org/10.3390/en14020319

Jolliffe, I. T. (2002). *Principal component analysis for special types of data*. Springer.

Liu, L., Wan, W., & Wu, Y. J. (2020). How nonlocal entrepreneurial teams achieve sustainable performance: The interaction between regional entrepreneurial ecosystems and organizational legitimacy. *Sustainability (Switzerland)*, *12*(21), 9237. https://doi.org/10.3390/su12219237

Liu, Y. (2020). The micro-foundations of global business incubation: Stakeholder engagement and strategic entrepreneurial partnerships. *Technological Forecasting and Social Change*, *161*, 120294. https://doi.org/10.1016/j.techfore.2020.120294

Lowitzsch, J., Hoicka, C. E., & van Tulder, F. J. (2020). Renewable energy communities under the 2019 European Clean Energy Package—Governance model for the energy clusters of the future? *Renewable and Sustainable Energy Reviews*, *122*, 109489. https://doi.org/10.1016/j.rser.2019.109489

Mataczyńska, E., & Kucharska, A. (Eds.) (2020). *Klastry energii: Regulacje, teoria i praktyka*. Wydawnictwo Naukowe Instytutu Polityki Energetycznej im. I. Łukasiewicza. https://www.instytutpe.pl/wp-content/uploads/2019/09/Klastry-energii.-Regulacje-teoria-i-praktyka.pdf

Luken, R., & Castellanos-Silveria, F. (2011). Industrial transformation and sustainable development in developing countries. *Sustainable Development*, *19*(3), 167–175.

Manowska, A., Osadnik, K. T., & Wyganowska, M. (2017). Economic and social aspects of restructuring Polish coal mining: Focusing on Poland and the EU. *Resources Policy*, *52*, 192–200. https://doi.org/10.1016/j.resourpol.2017.02.006

Markusen, A. (1996). Sticky places in slippery space: A typology of industrial districts. *Economic Geography*, *72*(3), 293–313.

Martin, R., & Sunley, P. (2017). Towards a developmental turn in evolutionary economic geography? In D. Kogler (Ed.), *Evolutionary economic geography* (pp. 8–28). Routledge.

Meshkov, I. (2019). Analysis of cluster initiatives in the energy sector of the EU. In V. Litvinenko (Ed.), Youth technical sessions proceedings (pp. 45–49). Taylor & Francis Group. https://doi.org/10.1201/9780429327070-7

Micek, D., Kocór, M., Worek, B., & Szczucka, A. (2021). *Społeczne uwarunkowania funkcjonowania klastrów energii w Polsce: Raport podsumowujący analizę studium przypadku wybranych klastrów: Cz. 3.* Ministerstwo Rozwoju, Pracy i Technologii, Akademia Górniczo-Hutnicza im. Stanisława Staszica w Krakowie, Narodowe Centrum Badań Jądrowych. https://www.er.agh.edu.pl/media/filer_public/66/cb/66cb3fd2-854d-47c5-baaa-c2952fb8e639/raport_spoleczne_uwarunkowania_funkcjonowania_klastrow_energii_w_polsce.pdf

Ministry of Climate and Environment (2021). *Energy policy of Poland until 2040* (EPP2040). https://www.gov.pl/web/climate/energy-policy-of-poland-until-2040-epp2040

Mirowski, T., & Kubica, K. (2016). The role of biomass in energy clusters. *Polityka Energetyczna*, *19*(4), 125–138.

Mucha-Kuś, K., Sołtysik, M., Zamasz, K., & Szczepańska-Woszczyna, K. (2021). Coopetitive nature of energy communities—The energy transition context. *Energies*, *14*(4). https://doi.org/10.3390/en14040931

Nadeem, T. B., Siddiqui, M., Khalid, M., & Asif, M. (2023). Distributed energy systems: A review of classification, technologies, applications, and policies. *Energy Strategy Reviews*, *48*, 101096.

North, D. C. (2010). *Understanding the process of economic change*. Princeton university press.

O'Connor, A., Stam, E., Sussan, F., & Audretsch, D. B. (2017). Entrepreneurial ecosystems: The foundations of place-based renewal. In *Entrepreneurial ecosystems: Place-based transformations and transitions* (pp. 1–21). Springer International Publishing.

O'Kane, P., Smith, A., & Lerman, M. P. (2021). Building transparency and trustworthiness in inductive research through computer-aided qualitative data analysis software. *Organizational Research Methods*, *24*(1), 104–139. https://doi.org/10.1177/1094428119865016

Oinas, P., Trippl, M., & Höyssä, M. (2018). Regional industrial transformations in the interconnected global economy. *Cambridge Journal of Regions, Economy and Society*, *11*(2), 227–240.

Ostrom, E. (2010). Beyond markets and states: Polycentric governance of complex economic systems. *American Economic Review*, *100*(3), 641–672.

Sanguansat, P. (2012). *Principal component analysis. InTech.*

Saris, W. E., & Gallhofer, I. N. (2014). Design, evaluation, and analysis of questionnaires for survey research. John Wiley & Sons.

Schwabe, J. (2024). Regime-driven niches and institutional entrepreneurs: Adding hydrogen to regional energy systems in Germany. *Energy Research & Social Science*, *108*, 103357.

Simsek, Z., & Veiga, J. F. (2001). A primer on internet organizational surveys. *Organizational Research Methods*, *4*(3), 218–235.

Simsek, Z., & Veiga, J. F. (2000). The electronic survey technique: An integration and assessment. *Organizational Research Methods*, *3*(1), 93–115.

Smith, A., Stirling, A., & Berkhout, F. (2004). *Governing sustainable industrial transformation under different transition contexts.* In *Governance for Industrial Transformation, Proceedings of the 2003 Berlin Conference on the Human Dimensions of Global Environmental Change* (pp. 113–132). https://www.academia.edu/download/30715730/10.1.1.197.8530.pdf

Sołtysik, M., & Kozakiewicz, M. (2018). Selected optimization issues in the energy clusters. *Rynek Energii*, *2018*(3), 9–13.

Speck, S., Paleari, S., Tagliapietra, S., & Zoboli, R. (2023). *Investments in the sustainability transition: Leveraging green industrial policy against emerging constraints.* EEA European Environment Agency. https://doi.org/10.2800/451268

Spigel, B. (2022). Examining the cohesiveness and nestedness entrepreneurial ecosystems: Evidence from British FinTechs. *Small Business Economics*, *59*(4), 1381–1399.

Surwillo, I. (2022). Energy clusters in Poland: Towards diffused green energy communities. In F. Karimi, & M. Rodi (Eds.), *Energy transition in the Baltic Sea region* (pp. 185–204). Routledge.

Szewranski, S., Kachniarz, M., Sylla, M., Swiader, M., & Tokarczyk-Dorociak, K. (2019). Spatio-temporal assessment of energy consumption and socio-economic drivers in rural areas in Poland. *Engineering for Rural Development*, *18*, 1372–1378.

Tauron Polska Energia (2024). *Energy Clusters in the activities of the Ministry of Energy*. https://www.tauron.pl/tauron/o-tauronie/tauron-dla-otoczenia/klastry-energii

Trejo-Nieto, A. (2021). Green industrial policies for sustainability and resilience. In R. Brears (Ed.), *The Palgrave encyclopedia of sustainable resources and ecosystem resilience* (pp. 1–18). Springer International Publishing. https://doi.org/10.1007/978-3-030-67776-3_33-1

Wawrzyniak, K., Walkowiak, S., & Cetnarski, R. (2021). Elastyczność w sieci OSD jako kluczowy komponent transformacji energetycznej. *Energetyka Rozproszona, 5–6*, 75–90.

Williamson, O. E. (2000). The new institutional economics: Taking stock, looking ahead. *Journal of Economic Literature*, *38*(3), 595–613.

Wiseman, H. J. (2023). Energy governance models. In G. Bellantuono, L. Godden, H. Mostert, H. Wiseman, & H. Zhang (Eds.), *Handbook of energy law in the low-carbon transition* (pp. 41–64). https://doi.org/10.1515/9783110752403-010

Wright, A. L., Middleton, S., Hibbert, P., & Brazil, V. (2020). Getting on with field research using participant deconstruction. *Organizational Research Methods*, *23*(2), 275–295.

Zukauskaite, E., Trippl, M., & Plechero, M. (2017). Institutional thickness revisited. *Economic Geography*, *93*(4), 325–345.

4 Sustainable Industrial Transformation in Polish Energy Clusters in the Context of International Cluster Policies

4.1 Development Phase of Polish Energy Clusters – Research Findings

Identification of the Development Phase of Polish Energy Clusters

In line with the research framework (Figure 3.1) that emphasizes the profiling of cluster development phases, we used a taxonomic k-means clustering technique. This approach allows to identify the groups of clusters with similar characteristics reflecting the development phase (profiles) of these sustainable industrial transformation initiatives in the energy field. Since these groups are termed "clusters" in the k-means analysis, when reporting the findings, we will use an alternative term "group" to avoid confusion since energy clusters are the main objects of our investigations.

Based on the taxonomic approach, the respective local initiatives can be categorized into evolutionary or life-cycle stages with unique characteristics related to governance and energy-sustainable industrial transformation (ESIT). These findings will also be interpreted and discussed using a qualitative content analysis of secondary data sources, interview material, and open survey questions to improve the understanding of the phenomenon studied.

As part of the k-means analytical procedure, the number of distinct cluster groups was determined using the scree plot, which belongs to the techniques of principal component analysis and classification (Aczel & Sounderpandian, 2018). The scree plot indicated a flattening of the line after the second factor, which determined the number of two groups (Cattell, 1966) (Figure 4.1). The first two distinguished factors explain 53% of the total variability in the sample, with all four factors whose eigenvalues were greater than 1 accounting for 72% of the total variance, which exceeds the required threshold of 70% (Cattell, 1966).

According to analysis of variance (F and p statistics values), the most differentiating variables in the sample of energy clusters are of governance type (Table 4.1). Primarily, they include the intensity of collaboration

DOI: 10.4324/9781003623540-5

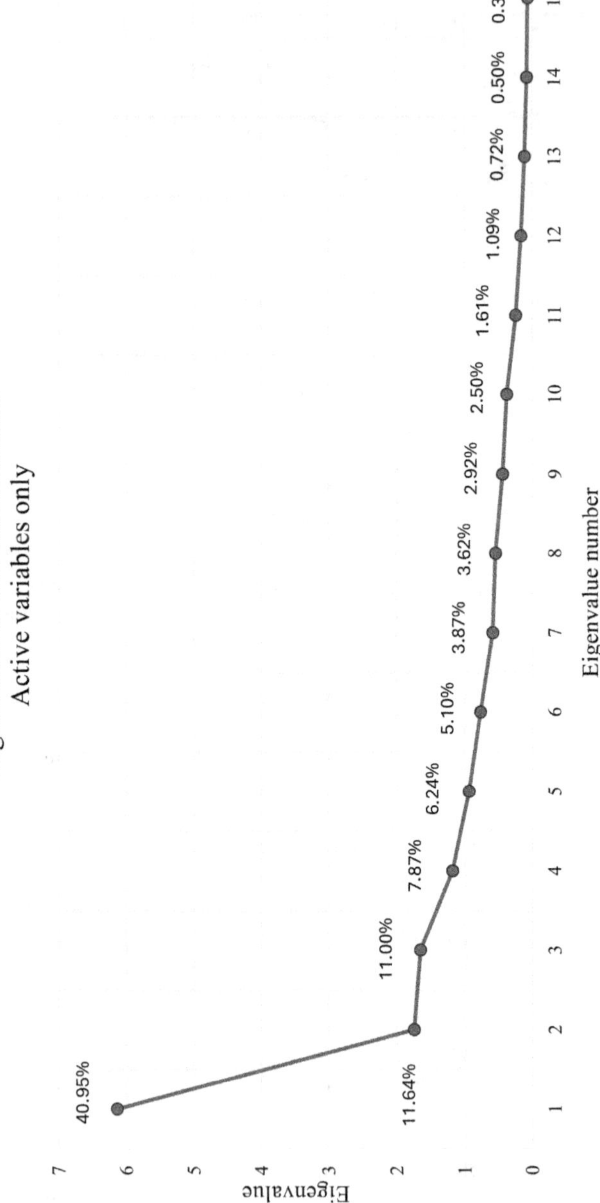

Figure 4.1 Scree plot with eigenvalues for determining the number of groups in the k-means analysis

Table 4.1 Analysis of variance in the sample researched

Variable	*Between SS*	*Df*	*Within SS*	*Df*	*F*	*Signif. p*
ESITRES	10.612	1	31.388	41	13.862	0.000
ESITEN	12.346	1	29.654	41	17.069	0.000
ESITIN	13.781	1	28.219	41	20.023	0.000
ESITRD	6.096	1	35.904	41	6.961	0.012
GLEAD	28.035	1	13.965	41	82.311	0.000
GDON	6.925	1	35.075	41	8.095	0.007
GDCN	5.960	1	36.040	41	6.780	0.012
GDRN	8.494	1	33.506	41	10.394	0.003
GCLG	26.717	1	15.283	41	71.676	0.000
GCC	28.537	1	13.463	41	86.907	0.000
GCCF	4.138	1	37.862	41	4.481	0.040
GCRD	19.050	1	22.950	41	34.033	0.000
GINT	7.788	1	34.212	41	9.333	0.003
GSTR	0.173	1	41.827	41	0.169	0.683
GPF	1.938	1	40.063	41	1.983	0.167

Source: own research.

between companies (GCC), the type of leadership in a cluster (GLEAD), the intensity of collaboration with local government units (GCLG) and research entities (GCRD), as well as the number of research entities in a cluster (GDRN). The sources of significant differentiation are also variables describing energy-sustainable industrial transformation, namely, the pursuit of innovation (ESITIN), the investment of the company in environmental technologies (ESITEN), and the adoption of renewable energy sources (ESITRES). These results point to the importance of governance type, in terms of leadership and collaboration, in particular collaboration among cluster companies, local government, and research entities. The latter is also associated with the number of research entities. The respective governance indicators can be perceived as substantively contributing to the energy industrial transformation.

Three out of four proxies for ESIT have proved to contribute significantly to the sample variation, and these include input indicators of innovation pursuit (ESITIN) and company investment in environmental technologies (SEIEN), and the output indicator of RES adoption (ESITRES). The revealed sources of governance and ESIT variance from the sample demonstrate a coherent explanatory potential to highlight the cluster development phase and the efficiency of related public policies.

The weakest variation in the sample is caused by factors that describe entrepreneurial activity (GSTR), public financing (GPF), and the level of formalization of cluster companies' collaboration (GCCF). These results suggest that clusters achieve different development phases not due to the entrepreneurial activity of startups, but to the activity of established firms. However, it can also be treated as a sign of a lower internal innovation potential and reliance on threshold and standard technologies or on external sources of knowledge (GINT). The latter variable is statistically significant and represents a stronger differentiating factor (Table 4.1). The type of financing and the role of public sources of financing (GPF) do not differentiate the sample. This condition was commonly reported as crucial development barrier and a weakness of a respective public policy by the initiatives surveyed.

The analysis of the group means (Table 4.2) allows the identification of the configuration of variables that represent two stages of cluster development within the sample investigated. It also enables the delineation of their unique profiles with detailed characteristics.

Two identified groups are almost equal by group membership, namely, groups Group 1 includes 22 entities (51% of the sample) and Group 2 covers 21 subjects (49% of the sample). They reveal considerable differences in mean values, both for sustainable industrial transformation and for governance characteristics. However, it should also be noted that both score rather low or moderately according to the original scales of the ESIT and governance variables (Table 4.3). This indicates that even though the differences among the groups are statistically significant and we can determine their distinct development stages, the referred stages are rather initial than growth or advanced stages of the cluster life cycle or evolution.

In terms of energy-sustainable industrial transformation (ESITRES, ESITEN, ESITIN, ESITRD), Group 1 is distinguished by relatively higher means

Table 4.2 Group means for two development stages of energy cluster initiatives

Variable	*Group No. 1 (22 cases, 51% of the sample)*		*Group No. 2 (21 cases, 49% of the sample)*		*U (p value adjusted)*
	Mean stn.	*Mean orig.*	*Mean stn.*	*Mean orig.*	
ESITRES[a]	0.485	0.409	−0.509	0	**<0.005**
ESITEN[a]	0.524	0.864	−0.548	0.333	**<0.005**
ESITIN[a]	0.553	0.500	−0.579	0	**<0.001**
ESITRD	0.368	0.500	−0.385	0.143	**<0.05**
GLEAD[a]	0.789	0.955	−0.827	0.143	**<0.001**
GDON[c]	0.392	1.864	−0.411	1	**<0.005**
GDCN[c]	0.364	1.727	−0.381	1	**<0.005**
GDRN[c]	0.434	1.682	−0.455	1.095	**<0.005**
GCLG[c]	0.770	3.727	−0.807	1.619	**<0.001**
GCC[c]	0.796	3.364	−0.834	1.238	**<0.001**
GCCF[c]	0.303	1.818	−0.318	1.238	0.054
GCRD[c]	0.650	2.682	−0.681	1.095	**<0.001**
GINT[c]	0.416	1.773	−0.436	1.048	**<0.005**
GSTR[c]	0.062	1.273	−0.065	1.191	0.480
GPF[b]	−0.207	1.773	0.217	2.143	0.174

Notes: N = 43; U – Mann-Whitney U test; [a] – binary variable 0,1; [b] – Likert scale 1–3; [c] – Likert scale 1–5; mean orig. – mean for data in original scales; mean stn. – mean for the standardized data.

Source: own research.

Table 4.3 Descriptive statistics of ESIT and governance indicators for two groups of clusters

Variable	*Group No. 1 (22 cases, 51% of the sample)*		*Group No. 2 (21 cases, 49% of the sample)*	
	*N**	*%*	*N**	*%*
ESITRES[a]	13 (0)	59	21 (0)	100
	9 (1)	41	1 (0)	0
ESITEN[a]	3(0)	14	14 (0)	67
	19 (1)	86	7 (1)	33
ESITIN[a]	11 (0)	50	21 (0)	100
	11 (1)	50	0 (1)	0
ESITRD[a]	11 (0)	50	18 (0)	86
	11 (1)	50	3 (1)	14
GLEAD[a]	1 (0)	95	18 (0)	86
	21(1)	5	3 (1)	14
GDON[c]	14 (<15 units; 1)	64	21 (1)	100
	3 (15–19 units; 2)	13	0 (2)	0
	1 (20–34 units; 3)	5	0 (3)	0
	2 (35–50 units; 4)	9	0 (4)	0
	2 (>50 units; 5)	9	0 (5)	0
GDCN[c]	14 (<10 firms; 1)	64	21 (1)	100
	5 (10–20 firms; 2)	26	0 (2)	0
	0 (21–30 firms; 3)	0	0 (3)	0
	1 (31–40 firms; 4)	5	0 (4)	0
	1 (>40 firms; 5)	5	0 (5)	0
GDRN[c]	9 (0 R&D entities; 1)	41	18 (0)	86
	12 (1 R&D entity; 2)	54	3 (1)	14
	0 (2 R&D entities; 3)	0	0 (2)	0
	1 (3 R&D entities; 4)	5	0 (3)	0
	0 (>3 R&D entities; 5)	0	0 (4)	0
GCLG[c]	0 (1)	0	12 (1)	57
	0 (2)	0	6 (2)	29
	0 (3)	46	2 (3)	9
	8 (4)	36	1 (4)	5
	5 (5)	18	0 (5)	0
GCC[c]	1 (1)	5	18 (1)	86
	1 (2)	5	1 (2)	5
	10 (3)	45	2 (3)	9
	9 (4)	40	0 (4)	0
	1 (5)	5	0 (5)	0

(Continued)

Table 4.3 (Continued)

Variable	*Group No. 1 (22 cases, 51% of the sample)*		*Group No. 2 (21 cases, 49% of the sample)*	
	*N**	*%*	*N**	*%*
GCCF[c]	11 (informal collaboration; 1)	50	16 (1)	76
	8 (formal agreements; 2)	36	5 (2)	24
	1 (joint investment; 3)	5	0 (3)	0
	0 (joint ventures; 4)	0	0 (4)	0
	2 (company integration; 5)	9	0 (5)	0
GCRD[c]	5 (1)	23	19 (1)	90
	5 (2)	23	2 (2)	10
	4 (3)	18	0 (3)	0
	8 (4)	36	0 (4)	0
	0 (5)	0	0 (5)	0
GINT[c]	13 (1)	59	20 (1)	95
	3 (2)	14	1 (2)	5
	4 (3)	18	0 (3)	0
	2 (4)	9	0 (4)	0
	0 (5)	0	0 (5)	0
GSTR[c]	18 (no startups; 1)	82	19 (1)	90
	3 (1 startup; 2)	14	0 (2)	0
	0 (2 startups; 3)	0	2 (3)	10
	1 (3 startups; 4)	4	0 (4)	0
	0 (4 or more startups; 5)	0	0 (5)	0
	10 (informal coll.; 1)	45	7 (1)	33
	7 (formal coll.; 2)	32	4 (2)	19
	5 (capital coll.; 3)	23	10 (3)	48

Notes: N = 43; * – scale values in brackets; [a] – binary variable 0,1; [b] – Likert scale 1–3; [c] – Likert scale 1–5.

Source: own research.

compared to Group 2. Group 1 scores high in company investment in environmental technologies (ESITEN). As much as 86% of the entities bear this investment and hence pursue research and development (R&D) activity, compared to only 33% of Group 2 companies involved in this activity. Although only half of the Group 1 members engage in innovation pursuit (ESITIN) and partnership with R&D entities (ESITRD), the advantage over the second cluster is even higher. Group 1 members do not engage in developing innovation at all, while their R&D partnerships are only marginal and reported by 14% of this group. A notable difference refers to the adoption of RES. Less than half of the initiatives in Group 1

(41%) report RES of at least 21% in total energy production, while this threshold has not been met by any of the Group 2 participants. Therefore, the adoption of RES, as the output indicator of ESIT, is only present in Group 1 membership, demonstrating its greater advancement of sustainable industrial transformation in energy provision at the local level.

The two identified classes of local energy initiatives are also different with respect to most governance indicators, including cluster leadership (GLEAD), a complex variable of the density of participation (overall number of cluster participants/GDON/, number of companies/GDCN/, number of R&D entities/GDRN/), a complex variable of internal collaboration (with local government/GCLG/, companies/GCC/, R&D entities/GCRD/), and international knowledge transfer collaboration (GINT). Almost all Group 1 entities are led by companies as central tenants (95%) and only one organization belongs to the group of local government-led initiatives. An inverted proportion can be observed for Group 2 dominated by local government-led initiatives, with only three participants (14%) being firm-led.

The density of participation in Group 1 energy initiatives is stronger than in the case of those in Group 2. This concerns the overall number of participants (GDON), which counts 14 initiatives with less than 15 members, four initiatives with 15 to 34 members, two with 35 to 50 members, and two with more than 50 members. The same governance indicator for Group 2 shows exclusively entities of the smallest size, that is, under 15 participants. The density of companies (GDCN) in Group 1 is evidenced by 14 initiatives including less than 10 firms, five that embrace 10 to 20 firms, one with 31 to 40, and two subjects with more than 40 firms. This is in contrast with Group 2, where all organizations include less than 10 entities, often limited to only one company acting as a coordinator of the cluster rather than a producer or technology provider. Twelve initiatives in Group 1 include two R&D members, nine of them report no R&D participants, and one initiative boasts three R&D partners. In the case of Group 2, only three entities indicate one R&D participant while the remaining 18 subjects do not include R&D entities. The higher density and ESIT indicators in Group 1 and its distinct properties compared to Group 2 in this regard suggest that there is a positive association between the number of cluster participants and the input and output indicators of industrial transformation.

The governance from the angle of internal collaboration is also favorable in Group 1 compared to Group 2. The intensity of collaboration with local governments and between cluster companies scores above average, while the intensity of cooperation among companies and R&D organizations is close to the moderate (average) level of scale. External collaboration in Group 1 organizations, in terms of international knowledge sourcing, indicates a lower level of intensity. However, four initiatives report moderate collaboration, while two of them evaluate these relationships as strong. This contrasts with Group 2, where all the entities declare very weak (20 cases) and weak (one case) collaboration of this type. Like the density of participation, the characteristics of Group 1, in particular compared to Group 2, suggest a positive relationship between the level of collaboration and sustainable industrial transformation.

The differences between governance conditions covering the level of formalization of collaboration among companies (GCCF), entrepreneurial activity as a number of startups in a cluster (GSTR) and public financing (GPF) did not prove statistically significant (Table 4.2). Regarding the observed values of the formalization, companies in Group 1 are more prone to adopt formalization and the solutions toward capital integration. The latter formalization of cooperation does not exist among the organizations of Group 2 at all. The startups are marginally present in the sample, proving that this activity is largely based on the existing companies, and the energy initiatives do not form entrepreneurial ecosystems for new ventures supporting the energy transition process. In the sample, 37 organizations report that they do not have startups, while six host 1 to 3 new ventures (four of them belong to Group 1). Public financing is the only financial source in 17 cases, while in 11 cases it is used as one of the sources, and in 15 cases it is not available at all.

In addition, the profiles of resource potential (installation energy power/IEP/, population/POP/covered by the cluster area) and capability potential (duration of operations/AGE/) considerably differentiate organizations in two groups (Table 4.4). In all these aspects, the energy clusters in Group 1 demonstrate higher values compared to the organizations in Group 2. Regarding resource potential, Group 1 initiatives manage a higher installed energy and cover a larger population. In terms of capability potential, the history of operations (AGE) of Group 1 initiatives considerably exceeds this of the other group. At the same time, the two groups do not reveal statistically significant differences in the area of territorial reach (TER), representing the resource potential, and the scope of activities (ACT), which implies a capability potential.

Table 4.4 The group means for resource and capability potential of the energy clusters

Variable	*Group 1 (22 cases, 51% of the sample)*		*Group 2 (21 cases, 49% of the sample)*		*U (p value adjusted)*
	Mean stn.	*Mean orig.*	*Mean stn.*	*Mean orig.*	
IEP[a]	0.428	1.636	–0.448	1.095	**<0.005**
TER[a]	–0.026	1.909	0.027	1.952	0.826
POP[a]	0.369	3.000	–0.386	2.191	**<0.05**
AGE[a]	0.472	0.727	–0.495	0.238	**<0.005**
ACT[a]	0.137	1.727	–0.144	1.524	0.658

Notes: N = 43; U – Mann-Whitney U test; [a] – binary variable 0,1; [b] – Likert scale 1–3; [c] – Likert scale 1–5; mean orig. – mean for data in original scales; mean stn. – mean for data standardized.

Source: own research.

The Characteristics of Energy Cluster Groups Against Resource and Capability Potential

Based on the above analysis and the Euclidean distances, Group 1 is clearly distinguished from Group 2, demonstrating a higher advance in governance and related ESIT (Table 4.5).

The cluster means graph allows visualization of the configurations of variables in two groups and their profiles in terms of individual attributes (variable levels) (Figure 4.2).

The findings highlight two groups of cluster initiatives that strongly differ in the characteristics of governance and ESIT, with a few exceptions that refer to governance. Our theorizing developed in Chapters 1 to 3 suggests that the advancements of governance and ESIT mark development stages in the life cycles or evolution of the phenomena studied. Both groups scored predominantly at lower or middle levels of the original ESIT scales and governance indicators. This implies that two distinct governance characteristics represent rather initial (early) evolutionary stages. Referring to the development stages proposed by Colombelli et al. (2019), who identify a birth phase, intermediate phase, and a developed phase, we find Group 1 in an intermediate phase and Group 2 in a birth phase. This resonates with the development of density and collaboration determined in theory for the initial phases by Colombelli et al. (2019). Additionally, our approach corresponds to other criteria proposed by Brown and Mason (2017), including the intensity of entrepreneurial activity international links, and public financing.

The energy clusters in the intermediate stage of development have low to moderate density governance, considering the overall number of members, the number of companies, and the R&D entities. Their intensity of collaboration is above average or strong in the area of relationships with local government and between companies and moderate in the area of company links with R&D entities. They also reveal an incremental participation in international knowledge sourcing. Regarding the formalization of interfirm collaboration, intermediate-phase energy initiatives distinguish by adoption of ownership relationships and capital integration. This can contribute to strengthening the transformative potential of incumbent companies both in the area of energy provision and in the technological advancement toward RES.

Table 4.5 Euclidean distances between the groups of local energy clusters

Cluster	*Cluster No. 1*	*Cluster No. 2*
No. 1	0,000	1,121
No. 2	1,059	0,000

Source: own research.

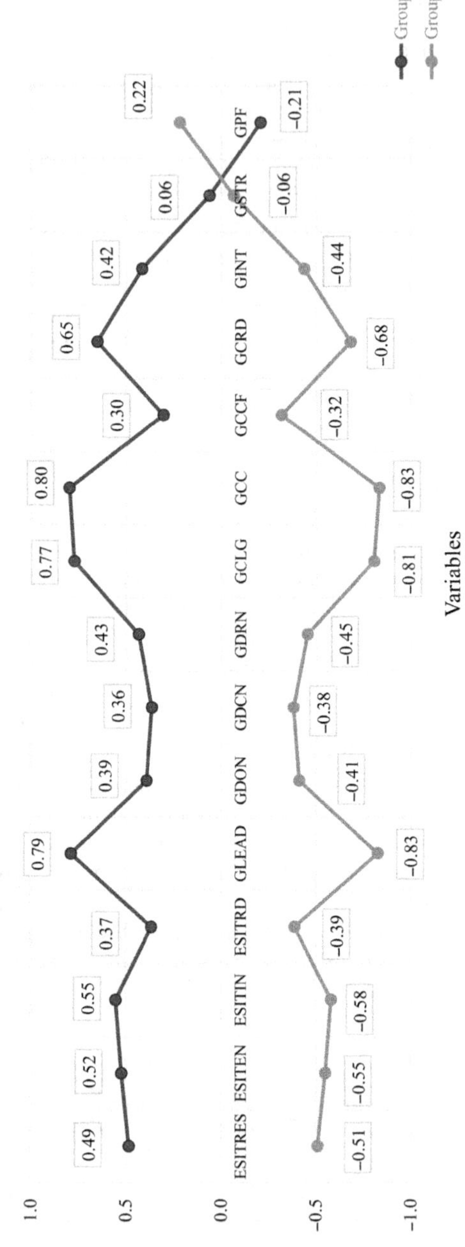

Figure 4.2 Plot of means for two groups of energy clusters; standardized values

However, the entities in this development phase marginally generate spin-offs or startups that would prove their own innovative efforts in the area of energy provision (only four organizations declare at least one startup). This can be explained by only a half of the initiatives involved in innovation activities and including an R&D entity in their organization. Moreover, the minor representation of new ventures implies external sources of environmental technologies rather than internal technological innovation. Ultimately, public financing as the only source predominates (45% of cases) or is one of the financial sources (32% of cases); that is, public involvement is present in 77% of subjects. Only 23% of the clusters rely on financial sources other than public support, predominantly on member fees. This funding structure can be considered as typical of an intermediate development stage, when public sources are overly present, and private sources remain marginal.

The governance characteristics are sufficiently favorable to contribute to at least medium levels of input factors for sustainable industrial transformation. The latter factors, in turn, can improve the ESIT output indicator measured by the share of RES in overall energy production. The intermediate phase differentiates by the adoption of RES on a considerable scale, which is only present among the organizations in this group and is not evidenced in the groups of the birth group at all. At the same time, RES adoption is only pursued by less than half of the initiatives that feature this development phase.

Such a configuration of characteristics represents an interlinked, mutually reinforcing a mixture of conditions and effects that support not only balancing energy provision at the local level, but also industrial transformation in this economic area. However, the levels of governance and ESIT indicators classify this development stage as intermediate rather than a developed stage (Brown & Mason, 2017; Colombelli et al., 2019).

These characteristics of the intermediate development phase resonate with the resource and capability potential of the respective energy initiatives (Table 4.6). Regarding resource potential, their installed energy power (IEP) is predominantly lower than 5 megawatts (50% of initiatives); however, 36% of these entities govern the power of 5 to 50 megawatts, and 14% more than 50 megawatts. In terms of TER, 64% of the intermediate phase organizations cover the territory of 1 to 5 communes, while 36% represent one county. This is associated with the population covered (POP), whereby 50% of this cluster falls between 20,000 and 50,000 inhabitants, 9% is below 20,000, and 41% exceeds 50,000. The capability potential resulting from the duration of operation (AGE) shows a longer record of experience (73% of organizations established in 2016–2018) rather than a shorter history (27% of organizations started in 2021–2023). A dominant share of 55% of these clusters focus on one activity, while 18% perform two areas, and 27% conduct three or more fields of operations.

The energy clusters in the early stage of development adopt low-density governance with respect to the overall number of members, the number of

Table 4.6 Descriptive statistics for the resource and capability potential of the energy initiatives in the intermediate and birth phases

Variable	*Clusters in the intermediate phase (22 cases, 51% of the sample)*		*Clusters in the birth phase (21 cases, 49% of the sample)*	
	*N**	*%*	*N**	*%*
IEP[a]	11 (<5 megawatts; 1)	50	19 (1)	90
	8 (5–50 megawatts; 2)	36	2 (2)	10
	3 (>50 megawatts; 3)	14	0 (3)	0
TER[a]	10 (1–3 communes; 1)	46	6 (1)	28
	4 (4–5 communes; 2)	18	10 (2)	48
	6 (country; 3)	36	5 (3)	24
POP[a]	2 (<20,000; 1)	9	6 (1)	29
	5 (20,000–50,000; 2)	23	7 (2)	33
	6 (50,000–100,000; 3)	27	6 (3)	29
	9 (>100,000; 4)	41	2 (4)	9
AGE[a]	6 (2016–2018; 1)	27	16 (1)	76
	14 (2021–2023; 2)	73	5 (2)	24
ACT[a]	12 (1 activity; 1)	55	10 (1)	48
	4 (2 activities; 2)	18	11 (2)	52
	6 (3 or more activities; 3)	27	0 (3)	0

Notes: N = 43; * – scale values in brackets; [a] – binary variable 0,1; [b] – Likert scale 1–3; [c] – Likert scale 1–5; mean orig. – mean for data in original scales; mean stn. – mean for data standardized.

Source: own research.

companies, and R&D entities. The intensity of their collaboration with local government, companies, and R&D entities is very weak or weak. Similarly, their involvement in international knowledge sourcing is at a very low level. The birth-phase energy initiatives report primarily informal collaboration among companies and, to some extent, a formal collaboration. However, their company tenants do not engage in joint investment or capital ownership to increase the resource potential in the area of energy provision and their technological transformation towards RES.

The entities in this development phase marginally generate spin-offs or startups that would prove their own innovative efforts in the area of energy provision (only two organizations report three startups included). This can be caused by the fact that only a small share of these organizations invest in environmental technologies, there are no entities pursuing innovation, and there is only incremental membership of R&D entities. The birth stage of energy cluster development does not represent an entrepreneurial ecosystem for new ventures and future growth based on internal innovation activity. Public financing as the only or one of the financing sources is present in 52% cases, while other financing is used by 48% of initiatives. Public participation in this development stage is lower than that observed in the intermediate phase.

This evidence does not comply with the theoretical assumptions regarding the early development phases being heavily dependent upon the governmental sources rather than using private sources or being self-sufficient. Relatively low public involvement is not a proof of self-sufficiency and strong private engagement on the commercial basis. It rather represents a growth barrier in the conditions of underdeveloped structures and high investment needs that have to rely upon limited private sources, predominantly from member fees.

The respective unfavorable characteristics of the birth development stage provide a limited contribution to distributed energy-focused sustainable industrial transformation. Organizations at this stage of development do not adopt RES at all or they do not use it on a considerable scale. This can be explained by lack of innovation activity, a small share of companies investing in environmental technologies, and a representation of an R&D entity reported by only one initiative. To sum up, this configuration of governance and ESIT indicators supports the identification of the referred organizations with the earlier evolution phase, that is a birth stage (Brown & Mason, 2017; Colombelli et al., 2019).

The features reported for the development stage of the birth correspond to the resource and capability potential of the respective energy cluster organizations (Table 4.6). In terms of resource potential, their IEP is predominantly within the lowest range of less than 5 megawatts (90% of the initiatives), with only 10% falling between 5 and 50 megawatts. The TER is smaller than for the clusters in the intermediate phase, since 76% of them cover 1 to 5 communes, although this difference has not proved statistically significant (Table 4.4). The related population covered (POP) is also smaller since only 9% operate on an area of more than 100,000 inhabitants. The capability potential of experience based on the history of operations (AGE) is limited (24% of the organizations established in 2016–2018 and 74% started in 2021–2023). The scope of activities is narrower than in the intermediate group since 100% organizations perform one and two activities and none executes three or more fields.

Barriers and Drivers of the Energy Clusters in the Intermediate and Birth Development Phases

Table 4.7 indicates the main economic barriers articulated by the total sample and the sub-samples in different phases of development. These findings point to the dominant capital shortages reported by 40 entities. Only one organization pointed out no barriers, one indicated access to technology exclusively, and one subject emphasized access to distribution infrastructure as the only issue. Other important barriers, bound to capital shortages in individual indications, included access to infrastructure, technology, and competent human resources.

Although statistically insignificant (chi square; $p = 0.426$), we can observe some differences in the area of barriers to economic development between the groups in the intermediate and birth phases (Table 4.7). In

Table 4.7 Economic barriers reported by energy cluster initiatives in different development phases

Type of development barrier	*N for the intermediate phase (Group 1)*	*N for the birth phase (Group 2)*	*Row totals*
Capital	11	11	22
Capital, infrastructure	2	3	5
No barriers	0	1	1
Capital, human resources	3	4	7
Capital, technology	1	0	1
Capital, technology, infrastructure, human resources	2	0	2
Capital, technology, human resources	1	0	1
Technology	1	0	1
Capital, technology, infrastructure	1	0	1
Infrastructure	0	1	1
Totals	22	21	43

Notes: chi square for type of barrier and development phase – 10.169; p = 0.426.
Source: own research.

the birth phase, cluster initiatives indicate only capital, infrastructure, and human resource drawbacks. The unmet needs of the organizations in the intermediate phase are more extensive, since they also emphasize technological needs, while this aspect has not been acknowledged by any of the birth phase entities. This suggests that birth phase clusters, which do not engage in innovation activity and invest incrementally in environmental technologies, do not recognize these knowledge-related needs. They require the threshold capital and infrastructure to build their operations rather than to upgrade them through technological advancement and innovation. Consequently, intermediate-phase organizations reveal the needs related to upgrade and further growth.

The respondents were also asked to evaluate the legal conditions of the energy groups by expressing their opinions according to the 5-point Likert scale, where a value of 1 denoted highly unfavorable conditions and 5 denoted highly favorable conditions (Table 4.8). The general evaluation derived from the responses of the whole group (43 units) is moderate (18 responses for value 3), unfavorable (14 responses for value 2), or highly unfavorable (nine indications of value 1). Two respondents evaluated these legal conditions as favorable (value 4), but none of them perceived these conditions as highly favorable (value 5).

Table 4.8 Legal conditions evaluated by energy cluster initiatives

Evaluation of legal conditions Likert 1–5	*N for the intermediate phase (Group 1)*	*N for the birth phase (Group 2)*	*Row totals*
3	6	12	18
4	2	0	2
2	9	5	14
1	5	4	9
Totals	22	21	43

Notes: chi square for evaluation of legal conditions and development phase – 5.234; p = 0.156.
Source: own research.

The statistical chi-square test has not rejected independence of the evaluations of legal conditions and the development phase (Table 4.8). However, we can derive some observations from the evaluations of these groups shown in Table 4.8, as well as Figures 4.3 and 4.4.

The energy clusters in the intermediate phase are critics of legal arrangements and express either negative (nine cases) or strongly negative judgment (five cases), compared to the moderate attitude towards the legislatures (six cases) and their favorable evaluation (two cases only) (Figure 4.3, Table 4.8). No strongly positive evaluations were expressed. On the other hand, the cluster organizations in the birth phase perceive legal conditions in a more positive way, evaluating them as moderate (12 cases) or, to a smaller extent,

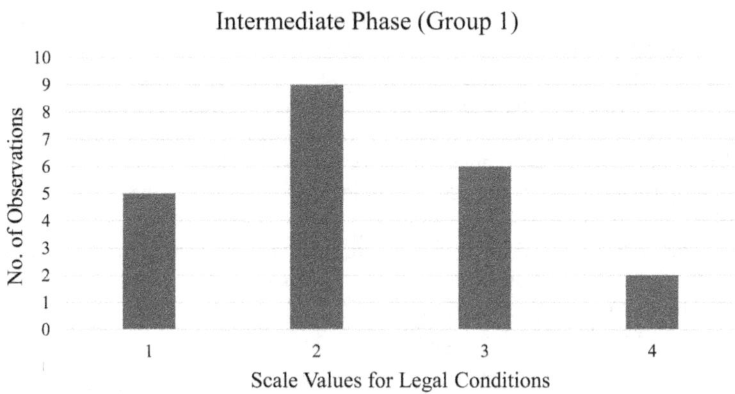

Figure 4.3 Legal conditions evaluated by energy cluster initiatives in the intermediate phase

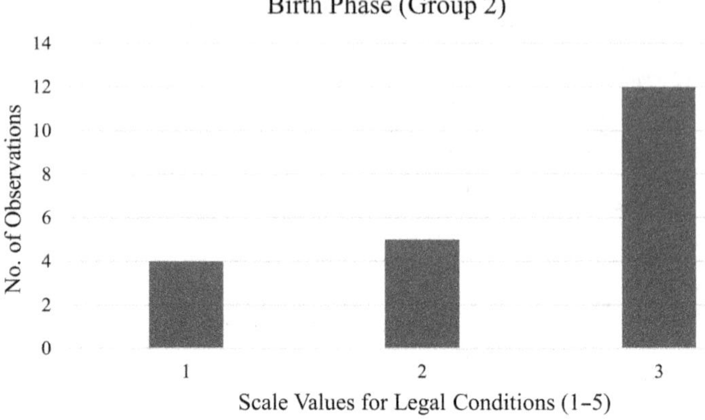

Figure 4.4 Legal conditions evaluated by energy cluster initiatives in the birth phase

unfavorable (five cases) and strongly unfavorable (four cases). However, no positive or very positive evaluations have appeared in this cluster group at all (Figure 4.4, Table 4.8).

The above comparison suggests that the intermediate group considers the legislatures as unfriendly to this group. At the same time, this group has longer experience of operations, pursues innovative and technological activities, and demonstrates achievements in RES adoption. This is a sign of policies that prevent the growth of clusters with capability potential, active operations, and predominantly coordinated by firm leaders. The respective judgments present legal provisions preventing the growth of company-centered clusters compared to those managed by territorial government.

The birth clusters, with local government as central tenants, have a moderate attitude to legal conditions. This approach can be explained by a shorter experience of the operations. Hence, their moderate attitude can be interpreted as being undecided or lacking experience to provide a distinct judgment. However, this group is even less prone to evaluate legal conditions as favorable or highly favorable, raising concerns whether the nascent clusters experience any support from the institutional environment at the country level (Figure 4.4, Table 4.8).

The above evaluations of the economic and legal conditions by groups in different development phases can be further explored in a more granular way by looking at the open responses of the sample researched (Table 4.9). Respondents provided their recommendations regarding economic and legal drivers of energy cluster growth.

The respondents have pointed to some major categories of drivers that are logically linked to the barriers reported in the findings. These recommendations primarily include the increase in funding and subsidies for

Table 4.9 Economic and legal drivers for energy clusters recommended by the respondents (paraphrases)

Recommendations from the intermediate phase initiatives (Group 1)	*Recommendations from the intermediate phase initiatives (Group 2)*
Amend the law on public procurement regarding the collaboration with territorial government within the cluster. No inquires or tenders are available.	To lower distribution fees for the infrastructures and facilities developed in energy clusters and dedicated to energy provision from RES.
Introduce the discounts for energy clusters in the field of electricity distribution that have been announced for several years.	
Introduce legislatures enhancing a comprehensive membership structure of energy clusters that should include territorial government, territorial government's capital companies, R&D entities, cultural and social organizations (non-profit partners), and private companies.	
Remove formal and legal barriers to the establishment of capital companies or associations linking territorial government and private companies.	
Provide financial instruments to support projects implemented by energy clusters.	
Ensure legal provisions that would abolish the obligation to apply the Public Procurement Law for the sale of energy within the cluster between members (in particular local government units and entrepreneurs).	
Free up energy trade between cluster members.	Improve legal conditions for the establishment of an energy cooperative by cities.
Provide support for cluster members; in particular, financial support.	Overcome the reluctance of energy operators to cooperate with the energy cluster, which is an entity necessary for the proper functioning of the energy system.
Ensure balance when it comes to small clusters; smaller ones are discriminated against and access to funds is only for designated ones.	
Improve access to funding and subsidies within the cluster for RES and other related purposes.	
Improve cooperation with the central government in building structures and developing cooperation and dialogue within the cluster.	
Improve legal conditions and introduce them in a timely manner. Suggestions and proposals stimulating the development of energy clusters have been repeatedly submitted, among others, through the National Chamber of Clusters. During the implementation of the cluster project, guidelines were developed; unfortunately, legislative changes are very slow and unsatisfactory.	
Ensure financial support, in particular, the long-announced support for cluster initiatives in the preinvestment and investment phase. Due to financial constraints, the cluster is at the stage of agreement and waiting for preinvestment support to prepare a development strategy.	

Source: own research.

clusters, as well as industrial policy legislatures that embed and organize the functioning of energy clusters in the general energy system. Importantly, the respondents articulate the rational purposes of the expected financing and legal changes and therefore prove their constructive attitude and readiness to pursue well-defined objectives and activities (Table 4.9). Moreover, we observe more recommendations and detailed opinions from the initiatives in the intermediate phase than in the birth phase, proving the accumulated experience and understanding of the organizational needs and industrial relations. The respondents in the intermediate group provide actionable policy recommendations and proposals for legal provisions. The smaller set of drivers articulated by the birth phase clusters overlaps with the demands of the intermediate counterparts. These calls emphasize lowering transaction costs; that is, the costs of distribution and coordination of exchanges with energy operators.

4.2 Recommendations for Economic Policy in the Context of the International Energy Cluster Experience

The recommendations for business and economic policy in this section stem from the results of our own primary research, but also embrace the conclusions of the review of secondary information sources and the international experience in developing distributed energy provision and energy cluster initiatives. In the following, we draw conclusions confronting the findings of our study with the research evidence and experience of international energy cluster policies, energy communities, and distributed energy programs.

Access to Finance and Other Areas of Direct Public Support

Based on our findings, in the area of financial support and subsidies, financial instruments are demanded with a clear target for particular projects implemented by energy clusters. The respondents also postulated discounts in the fees for electricity distribution. Furthermore, it has been emphasized that lowering distribution fees should concern infrastructures and facilities developed in energy clusters and dedicated to renewable energy provision. Therefore, access to funding is justified as a driver of RES adoption and development of projects related to RESs. Public financing can also act as a driver for the early-stage initiatives in preinvestment and investment activities. Without this financial enabler, the new cluster organizations will remain just signed agreements, waiting for preinvestment support, such as to develop the cluster strategy (Afeltowicz et al., 2024; Gryszczuk, 2024; Kuźniacki & Borek, 2023; Micek et al., 2021; Nadeem et al., 2023).

Taking into account the international experience, energy cluster initiatives and communities can draw resources from bottom-up stakeholders and participants in local government units (Deutz et al., 2024; Lowitzsch et al., 2020; Schwabe, 2024). The experience, organizational potential, and public trust of public utility companies in Germany make them natural leaders of networking necessary to establish and effectively operate energy projects (Lowitzsch et al., 2020; Speck et al., 2023). Local government units, private companies, individuals, households, and social organizations are crucial partners in these initiatives, contributing with investment, production, networking, and knowledge capacity (Debizet et al., 2022; Dreyfus & Suwa, 2022). Energy initiatives also develop from agreements to ownership structures of the respective stakeholders, such as in Denmark, France, and Germany (Lowitzsch et al., 2020; Nadeem et al., 2023; Tałan, 2021).

However, the development of distributed systems and related facilities requires a profound capital investment that typically cannot be incurred by local stakeholders in less developed countries, such as in countries of Central and Eastern Europe, including Poland (Dreyfus & Suwa, 2022; Gryszczuk, 2024; Kuźniacki & Borek, 2023; Lowitzsch et al., 2020; Schwabe, 2024; Tałan, 2021). Therefore, the system of financial country-level schema and central government should actively strengthen the support for these bottom-up initiatives through direct grants and subsidized loans or reliefs in financial burdens to operate the cluster. This support aligns with the provisions of the New Industrial Policy (NIP) of the European Union (EU) that promotes the bottom-up approach, including cluster initiatives, as well as technological advances for upgrading industrial structures, acknowledging the governance, social, and environmental goals (Gancarczyk & Ujwary-Gil, 2020; Gancarczyk et al., 2021, 2024).

The Roles of Lead Tenants and Structure of Membership

International institutions and recommendations for good practice emphasize the importance of member heterogeneity as value for building local networks and empowering and balancing various interests (European Parliament, 2012, 2018, 2019; Lowitzsch et al., 2020). One of the important findings of our study was the identification of the importance of the membership structure of energy clusters and their leadership. The legal provisions on the membership of the group and the founding entities, introduced in 2015, were open, allowing the leading roles of legal and natural persons from local governments and R&D entities. Our study was held at the turning point of legislative changes in this regard. The changes valid from the beginning of 2024 can be perceived as narrowing down the heterogeneity of membership. The new definition of the cluster emphasizes local governments as participants in the cluster agreement. This determines the central tenants or leaders of the initiatives, generating a sort of reluctance and disappointment on the part of businesses and other entities already involved in the initiatives. Although incumbent leadership can be retained in previously established organizations, the new wave of initiatives that conform to the referred legal amendment can ultimately displace the business models of energy clusters coordinated by firms. Furthermore, the amendment of the cluster agreement to reflect the new regulation will potentially be a prerequisite for being registered in the official records of the Energy Regulatory Office. This, in turn, can be a condition for bidding for public grants and subsidies (Gryszczuk, 2024).

Given our research findings, firm-led initiatives expose more technological and innovative capabilities towards a sustainable intermediate, including RES adoption. On the other hand, international institutions and good practice recommendations emphasize the importance of balanced ownership and decision making so that larger energy companies and operators did not take major stocks and bargaining power over local communities (European Parliament, 2012, 2018, 2019). There are approaches that exclude entities with market power and direct business interests in the energy industry from being involved in the ownership of cluster initiatives, such as the one observed in Germany or Denmark (Lowitzsch et al., 2020; Tałan, 2021). Following this, private companies can become cluster participants provided they do not expose market power, being micro and small entities, and the energy industry is not their main business field. These provisions secure the interest and decision power of local communities against the influence of commercial companies.

However, there also exist flexible solutions regarding the central coordinator and power balance in energy communities, such as in France (Debizet et al., 2022; Dreyfus & Suwa, 2022b). Energy communities can be governed by a broad array of economic and social issues, including larger competitors in the energy market. The value of power balance and ownership dispersion for the sake of social control should not be questioned. However, the issue of a public and social side that operates in isolation from business is its lack of competence in the area of technological progression and the innovative approach in products and business processes to meet the demands of industrial transitions. Therefore, the business side should be motivated by appropriate financial project-based incentives to participate in the clusters and be their active and creative participants (Gryszczuk, 2024; Kuźniacki & Borek, 2023).

Determining the Specificity and Purpose of Energy Cluster Initiatives in the Distributed Energy System

Energy cluster initiatives must address social and economic objectives including balancing the energy system, safety due to distributed energy that supports the overall energy supply or even substitutes this supply, environmental benefits by adopting RES, as well as savings in production and distribution in geographical proximity (Kuźniacki & Borek, 2023; Mataczyńska & Kucharska, 2020). These objectives make energy clusters synonymous with energy communities and cooperatives, which are local systems of distributed energy provision (Lowitzsch et al., 2020). However, cluster policies set out additional rationale of increasing competitiveness through specialization and innovation to ensure local development.

The energy clusters researched in this study share the referred social economic objectives of energy balance, safety, and environmental benefits. Still, they differ in development stage and related approach to innovation, technological advancement, and RES adoption to fulfill the rationales of competitiveness and innovation emphasized in NIP and the latest policy analyses (European Parliament, 2018; Gancarczyk & Ujwary-Gil, 2020; Trejo-Nieto, 2021). It would be useful to discriminate accordingly between the nature and purposes of existing energy cluster initiatives. One of the options is to distinguish between energy communities and energy clusters (Nadeem et al., 2023). Energy communities would address the threshold socioeconomic goals, such as energy balance, safety, and environmental protection, while innovation and competitiveness components would be optional for them. Energy clusters, in turn, would address both the threshold objectives and the upgradation through innovation and competitiveness. Currently, the energy clusters are at the cross-roads of infrastructural, industrial, innovation, R&D, and regional policies. Their unique nature as contributor to technological progression requires clarification and enhancement with related policies for technology and innovation development.

The existing structure of energy clusters in Poland reflects the above differences in rationales and the purposes they serve. Some of the authors distinguish between so-called grid-based clusters and virtual clusters (Kuźniacki & Borek, 2023). Grid clusters are small in scope by territoriality to perform real production and distribution in physical proximity and can be moderately prone to innovative and technological developments. Therefore, it would be advisable to provide incentives for their innovation and upgrading efforts. Virtual clusters cover larger territories, which prevents them from real economic activity for the sake of energy trading as auctions (Kuźniacki & Borek, 2023).

When discriminating between grid and virtual entities, it should be mentioned that Poland adopts an off-grid and grid-based as well as intermittent type of distributed energy system, including local energy initiatives. From the international perspective, grid and non-grid, as well as firm-load and intermittent-load models of distributed energy are applied. Grid options consist of local energy communities linked to the energy grid for storage and balancing purposes rather than operating these processes independently (off-grid system) (Nadeem et al., 2023). The grid model consists of a bidirectional flow of energy, from the producer to the energy operator and vice versa. Firm-load models are reliable for fully addressing the energy needs on demand. It represents an alternative power source when the electricity from the grid fails or during peak consumption hours. The intermittent-load system is not reliable to fully meet power needs on demand and requires energy storage either independently or with the use of grids. Renewable energy sources always require intermittent models.

We also observe hybrid solutions that combine these alternatives, such as in the wind and photovoltaic technologies in Australia. The choice between the models is primarily determined by spatial and climate conditions (Dreyfus & Suwa, 2022). If RES are not fully reliable as a constantly available source of energy, grid and intermitted options predominate. Moreover, large spatial distances in a country often impede access to the grid system and can justify non-grid distributed energy. Depending on the technology of distributed energy, the grid-based and intermittent systems are applied in Brazil for fuel cells, in Germany, India, and Algeria for photovoltaic. China adopts grid-off and firm system in biogas technology, while Denmark adopts wind and photovoltaic technology (Lowitzsch et al., 2020; Nadeem et al., 2023).

Structuring and Clarifying Industrial Relations in the Energy System

On the basis of our findings, in the area of industrial policy and related legislatures, there are postulates to organize industrial relations in the energy system among the key actors and integrate the clusters with the general energy system. The respondents recommend changes in the public procurement law to enhance collaboration with the territorial government involved in the cluster. Adequate legal provisions should abolish the obligation to apply the public procurement law for the sale of energy within the cluster, between its members, such local government units and entrepreneurs. Cluster initiatives directly call for freeing up energy trade between cluster members.

Another important growth stimulant would be the legislatures enhancing a broader membership structure of energy clusters that should link the key stakeholders of the territorial government, the capital companies of the territorial government, the R&D entities, non-profit and social organizations, and private companies. The legal provisions should remove formal and legal barriers to establishing capital companies or associations linking territorial government and private companies. An important legal provision to broaden the opportunities for developing a distributed energy system would be the improvement of the legal conditions for the establishment of energy cooperatives by cities.

Regarding industrial relations, our respondents observe unequal opportunities among cluster entities with differing potential. More balance is required to avoid discrimination of small groups in accessing development funds. Small clusters are so-called "grid-based clusters" that produce and exchange electrical energy in terms of real economy operations, as physical proximity allows this. Grid-based initiatives provide real savings for producers and distributors. This is in contrast with so-called virtual clusters, which operate on a larger territory, but the physical distance allows them to act as energy auction platforms rather than producers and distributors in the real economy.

Furthermore, the relationships between the existing and distributed systems and entities in energy provision (grid-based and virtual, incumbent energy operators and energy communities) require a careful consideration to specify the role and possible benefits (motivators, incentives) for this variety of stakeholders. These relationships should recognize conditions such as access to financing, ownership, and participation in governance (European Parliament, 2018; Lowitzsch et al., 2020; Trejo-Nieto, 2021).

The above recommendations emphasize the role of central government and national-level legislatures in organizing industrial relations, building industrial structures, and the institutions of collaboration and dialogue within the cluster and with its external stakeholders, such as incumbent energy operators. The quality and accuracy of legal institutions is crucial; however, its timely delivery represents another crucial recommendation and prospective driver of growth. The cluster initiatives surveyed emphasized that suggestions and proposals on development drivers have been repeatedly submitted. The National Chamber of Energy Clusters was one of the mediators in this process. During the consultations, the appropriate guidelines and recommendations were developed; however, the legislative changes proved very slow and unsatisfactory.

Legitimizing Energy Clusters as Recognized Parties in the Economic System and Energy Provision

Due to the grid system in Poland, there is a need to establish a collaboration between cluster initiatives with the system of incumbent energy operators. This can be a temporary phase of distributed energy development to a fully distributed system with production, distribution, and storage internal to energy communities or even individual prosumers. Other opinions and forecasts point to hybrid systems as a solution of the future. Considering the existing system and the ambiguity of its development, the relationships between clusters and energy operators require balancing of interests and establishing fair trading between the parties (European Parliament, 2018; Lowitzsch et al., 2020; Nadeem et al., 2023). The respondents admitted the reluctance of energy operators to collaborate, and this raises a problem of transaction costs in trading due to opportunistic behaviors of parties having a bargaining advantage. These transaction costs have been partially alleviated by recent legal amendments that clarified the reliefs in fees based on the level of energy self-sufficiency and RES adoption. On the other hand, the postulates to change the public procurement provisions and free the trade within clusters were not addressed in the respective amendments (Gryszczuk, 2024). Therefore, more policy instruments are needed to alleviate the internal and external transaction costs incurred by energy initiatives.

Tailoring the Policies and Related Support Instruments to the Needs of Clusters in Different Development Phases

Identifying cluster development phases in the Polish context is useful for adjusting policies to these unique conditions. Tailoring cluster policies to spatial and socioeconomic conditions, known as place-based approach, aligns with New Industrial Policy, as well as an institutional and evolutionary approach to industrial change and spatial development (Broadhurst et al., 2021; Gancarczyk & Ujwary-Gil, 2020; O'Connor et al., 2018). Our research evidenced two development phases of Polish energy clusters, unique by the characteristics of governance and sustainable industrial transformation. The value is not only in terms of understanding and explaining the level of development and upgradation, but also in normative conclusion as to the needs, drawbacks, and drivers perceived by the entities researched. Based on these findings and direct evaluations and recommendations, tailored policy instruments should be adopted.

A Comprehensive View of Public Governance Over the Energy Clusters as Embracing Technical, Legal, and Socioeconomic Institutions

The technical and legal governance of distributed energy and cluster initiatives predominates in existing research and policy. However, these naturally crucial conditions are insufficient to allow the proper functioning and growth of these phenomena. The important needs are access to capital, technologies, and reduction of transaction costs. The latter issue also depends on the ability to liaise and form local networks of institutional or social entrepreneurs engaged. At the local level, this can build trust and motivate efforts toward distributed energy. This study focuses on the socioeconomic governance and outcomes of ESIT rather than on the legal and technical aspects of the local energy initiatives. However, we also acknowledge the importance of higher levels of institutions and the necessary technical dimension. Increasingly, experts and researchers in the distributed energy field recognize socioeconomic governance as under-researched but a crucial element of the institutional structure and energy cluster policies. Therefore, we postulate integrative and interdisciplinary research and practice in RES and distributed energy to achieve sustainability.

The Importance of Country- and Regional-Level Institutions as Enablers of Energy Cluster Development

As follows from the opinions of the respondents, the local energy cluster initiatives are primarily affected by the laws and governmental agencies at the country level and indicate the expectation of support from this institutional level. Although they act in a particular environment of regional-level government, they either do not have any demands from this level of public administration, or their collaboration is efficient enough not to call for any improvements or articulate proposals. Therefore, cluster initiatives are subjects of national industrial policy, and they do not identify themselves with regional development frameworks. On the other hand, the spatial proximity featured by the participants makes them part of localized economic systems and regional development policies. The regional policy perspective should be more active in the support for energy communities, and the cluster members are advised to be more active in advocacy and articulating their interests against local and regional authorities.

Following the Benchmarks and Good Practice from International Institutions

Place-based national, regional, and local policies should be enriched with international experience and institutions (Lowitzsch et al., 2020). These international institutions include both legal provisions and good practice and routines developed in different settings (Tałan, 2021). The benefits of this comparative research include sharing good practices and standards with a possibility to adapt them to unique contexts (climate, political, and economic systems). Expert debate and research on Polish energy clusters rarely refers to the standards promoted as good practice regarding heterogeneity of members and governance from an ownership point of view. These experiences could bring about useful and actionable solutions to new legal arrangements and adjustments in the process of refining energy balancing and the search for renewable sources at the local level (Lowitzsch et al., 2020; Nadeem et al., 2023).

4.3 Discussion of the Results and Synthesis

Our research results enabled responses to the research questions related to our conceptual framework. Addressing Research Question 1, we have analyzed and identified development phases of Polish cluster policies in a multiscalar context at the local, country, and international levels. Following the research framework, we identified the characteristics of socioeconomic governance, according to the conditions described in the cluster policy-related literature. From the point of view of cluster properties, the respective policies have been identified as early stage. The national legislatures evolved from 2015 to 2024 to new provisions regarding membership, developing cluster agreement, and reporting, and to official register in the central government agency. Importantly, new regulations improve the distribution fee conditions, acknowledging the level of adoption of RES and self-sufficiency in energy provision. However, there are controversies as to narrowing membership rather than providing incentives for participant heterogeneity and improving participation of local social and economic actors. Moreover, some recognized patterns of good practice in the area of governance and ownership to ensure a balance among major stakeholders are less regarded.

Finally, there is ambiguity in understanding the purpose and expectations of the energy clusters, treated as an instrument in several policies, including infrastructural, industrial, regional, R&D, and innovation policies. This ambiguous status impedes a proper adjustment of industrial policy targets and support instruments. Considering the international experience of similar policies, pursued even from the 1980s of the 20th century, Polish cluster policies are young and dynamically evolving institutions that need to adapt to the frameworks set up by international legal provisions and should come from good practice accumulated in other socioeconomic contexts (Tałan, 2021). Additionally, regional-level policies should be recognized as complementary incentives for growth and activated given the spatial nature of the cluster initiatives.

In response to Research Question 2, we have detailed two development phases of energy cluster initiatives for sustainable industrial transformation in Poland, namely, the birth and intermediate phases. These were differentiated based on the characteristics of governance and ESIT indicators. The governance and its ESIT effect, combined with the properties of the resource and capability, provide a comprehensive profiling of two groups with different structural characteristics.

Research Question 3 referred to the barriers and drivers of energy cluster initiatives in Poland. On the basis of the response to the previous question, this study identified and described the energy cluster profiles. The latter can serve as a policy reference point by matching them with the assumptions made in the theory about effective governance and policy objectives regarding the advancement of ESIT. Furthermore, these profiles were enriched by direct evaluations of the main obstacles and indications of development drivers with the solutions proposed provided by the respondents.

Using the evolutionary and institutional approach to policy and industrial evolution, we provided both a granular description of the phenomena studied and also normative conclusions regarding the necessary improvements. Detailed inference from these findings and interpretation against international institutions and good practice are provided in Sections 4.1 and 4.2. A core message from these granular analyses is that clusters of different development phases share some common needs, in particular with respect to legal enablers, but also require policy approaches that match with their profiles (Benner, 2021; Colombelli et al., 2019).

Consequently, birth-stage clusters report shortages of capital, production, and distribution infrastructure, and coordination with energy operators. These barriers can be synthesized as basic financial and tangible capital shortages and excessive transaction cost. Correspondingly, the driving forces to the nascent clusters are access to financial capital and inclusion into the energy system. The latter is conditioned by a reduction of transaction costs, covering distribution fees and bargaining with the operators as trading partners. The intermediate phase clusters encounter similar threshold barriers but emphasize additional barriers and drivers that are important not only to local energy provision, and efficiency and safety of this supply. These obstacles and stimulants are relevant for the purposes of industrial policy, as they refer to upgrading, competitiveness, and industrial advancement.

Ultimately, Research Question 4 sought recommendations for energy cluster policies to enhance sustainable industrial transformation. These recommendations are detailed in Section 4.2. and display the following crucial areas. We advocate a granular approach in policy *ex ante* evaluations to plan strategies and tools, with a focus on evolutionary processes and different development phases of the policy subjects. Besides the development stage, this detailed approach should also acknowledge the purpose of cluster policies vis a vis the policies of local well-being and supply of threshold utilities. In addition, a match of the policy measures with the different barriers and drivers indicated by the initiatives is recommended. Furthermore, the upper levels of the policy of regions and countries should analyze and adopt the policy lessons from industrial relations at the local level. Country and territorial agencies and institutions should draw on comparative international experience and good practice and adapt this knowledge to their unique contexts (Broadhurst et al., 2021; O'Connor et al., 2018).

4.4 Contribution, Limitations, and Future Research Directions

Responding to the RQs specified above translates into the theory and economic policy of contribution of this research. *With regard to theoretical contribution, this research provides unique value by developing an analytical framework for cluster policies in the area of sustainable energy industrial transformation.* We proposed an empirically corroborated conceptual background rooted in institutional and evolutionary approaches, synthesized in Figure 4.1 (Benner, 2021; Grillitsch, 2015; Zukauskaite et al., 2017). This framework emphasizes three layers of institutions, including local governance, country, and international framework, that mutually influence the development of energy clusters and their achievement of ESIT (Acemoglu et al., 2002; Ostrom, 1986; Williamson, 2000). Based on this framework, we identify and explain the advancement of policies for energy cluster initiatives, as well as their drivers and obstacles.

The institutional and evolutionary approach gives valuable information on local development and industrial transformation processes, being a promising conceptual background for other studies of our research framework and method (Bohatkiewicz-Czaicka & Gancarczyk, 2025; Luken &

Castellanos-Silveria, 2011; Trejo-Nieto, 2021). This framework, corroborated with our empirical evidence, forms an analytical framework for future studies.

Our study uses a sample of representative observations to derive its generalizations. Although this is a small sample, it is still one of the few studies that uses a quantitative approach to make an argument and provide conclusions, given the predominance of case-based investigations (Afeltowicz et al., 2024; Micek et al., 2021; Surwillo, 2022; Tałan, 2021).

Regarding a contribution to policy and business practice, a crucial input is based on theory-based and empirical evidence-based recommendations regarding energy cluster policies. These actionable proposals for economic and legal measures were based on a detailed account of the energy, cluster-based, and sustainable development policies of the European Union (EU) (Dragan, 2020). Knowledge of the development phase, growth conditions (barriers and drivers), and actionable policy measures for cluster-based SIT in this study is informative for cluster administration and policymakers, and designing energy policy directions (Benner, 2021). The results of our study provide guidance on how to advance birth and intermediate stage groups with a tailored approach that recognizes their unique challenges and needs (Auerswald & Dani, 2017; Cantner et al., 2021).

Moreover, our findings contribute by identifying the conditions for a green transition at the bottom, local level, which is crucial to designing place-based policies (Dreyfus & Suwa, 2022). It should be assumed that these support measures will stimulate the development of local energy clusters and can be replicated in other locations for distributed energy systems. This approach could not only enhance distributed energy resource management and local grid resilience, but also create adaptable frameworks for sustainable energy transitions across regions with diverse socioeconomic and institutional profiles (Hassink, 2019).

This study is not free from limitations, which we specify and show how they were addressed in the area of method and interpretation of results. The small N sample allowed only an exploratory approach to the data and a more advanced causal analysis of the impact and effects was not possible. However, this sample is representative of the active population of clusters, and the results of statistical exploration enable responsible conclusions. Moreover, the explorative taxonomical approach applied is suitable for emergent phenomena, when many conditions should be considered. Exploring rich variables enables a granular approach to recognize the uniqueness of the respective policies and cluster growth processes rather than one average solution (Brown & Mason, 2017).

Focusing on a single country like Poland can be considered as limiting the possibility of generalization. However, the nuanced and context-dependent nature of research on energy clusters, policies, and industrial transformation predominates and is justified by the need for place-based policies (Broadhurst et al., 2021; Gancarczyk & Ujwary-Gil, 2020). Our decision to concentrate on a single country is motivated by the relevance of the problems and challenges of the industrial transition in this challenging context. Energy-intensive industries and a minor share of renewable sources in our country are accompanied by low social trust in green transformation and fear against the costs it can raise. The presented research enables a generalization for country policies undergoing an early stage and challenging industrial shift, relevant beyond national boundaries.

The context-specific approach is not only one of the major trends in the social science nowadays, but it is also one of the pillars of the NIP, gaining prominence both in the EU and worldwide. This policy acknowledges the place-based approach to designing and implementing territorial and industrial strategies, including smart specializations. Our monograph concentrates on an underresearched local level of industrial transition in a challenging context, and this focused approach can be also treated as a strength (Coenen & Truffer, 2012; Chembessi et al., 2024).

Regarding the scope of generalization, our analysis of the country context has been broadened with a review of international policies and experiences of energy communities. By situating our case study within this broader landscape, we provide insights that are context-specific and relevant to a wider discussion of energy clusters, cluster policies, and SIT processes globally. Furthermore, the policy measures and the cluster development conditions identified in our study represent a relevant experience for cluster-based industrial policies (Gancarczyk & Gancarczyk, 2013; Shakib, 2020). Therefore, we propose to treat them as evidence discussed and contributing to a wider perspective of international cluster policies through an institutional lens.

The limitations of this study inspire future research directions. These include expanding the empirical evidence to large-N samples to enable a statistical generalization. In addition, international comparative studies would enhance generalization and policy-related experience. These comparative studies can explore regions in a coherent institutional context, such as EU-wide studies, and in the differing contexts. In addition, investigating the experience of energy clusters in countries with different levels of development could be informative for tailored policies. Furthermore, since the presented research is unique in its focus on socioeconomic governance rather than technical and legal governance, we call for more studies in this area (Lowitzsch et al., 2020; Nadeem et al., 2023). Our focus on industrial transformation is related to the purpose of cluster policies, which is innovation, structural change, and competitiveness (Shakib, 2020). The existing rationale for energy communities and clusters is mainly in local energy provision, which brings economic, social, and environmental values for local entities. However, innovation and technological advancement are conditions that are necessarily localized and represent a condition for the respective values (Kuźniacki & Borek, 2023; Lowitzsch et al., 2020; Schwabe, 2024). Consequently, we call for research and policy to promote the niches of innovative cluster communities, including those that adopt and develop products and processes in the area of RESs (Grillitsch, 2015; Schwabe, 2024).

References

Acemoglu, D., Johnson, S., & Robinson, J. A. (2002). Reversal of fortune: Geography and institutions in the making of the modern world income distribution. *The Quarterly Journal of Economics, 117*(4), 1231–1294.

Aczel, A. D., & Sounderpandian, J. (2018). *Statystyka w zarzadzaniu*. Wydawnictwo Naukowe PWN.

Afeltowicz, Ł., Nawojczyk, M., & Tyrała, R. (2024). Entrepreneurial actions in energy transition: A study of three local energy clusters in Poland. *European Urban and Regional Studies, 31*(2), 132–148. https://doi.org/10.1177/09697764231179667

Auerswald, P. E., & Dani, L. (2017). The adaptive life cycle of entrepreneurial ecosystems: The biotechnology cluster. *Small Business Economics, 49*, 97–117.

Benner, M. (2021). Retheorizing industrial–institutional coevolution: A multidimensional perspective. *Regional Studies, 56*(3), 1–14.

Bohatkiewicz-Czaicka, J., & Gancarczyk, M. (2025). *Industrial clusters in international value chains: Conceptual advancement and empirical evidence from European ICT clusters*. Taylor & Francis.

Broadhurst, K., Ferreira, J., & Berkeley, N. (2021). Collaborative leadership and place-based development. *Local Economy, 36*(2), 149–163.

Brown, R., & Mason, C. (2017). Looking inside the spiky bits: A critical review and conceptualisation of entrepreneurial ecosystems. *Small Business Economics, 49*(1), 11–30.

Cantner, U., Cunningham, J. A., Lehmann, E. E., & Menter, M. (2021). Entrepreneurial ecosystems: A dynamic lifecycle model. *Small Business Economics, 57*(1), 407–423. https://doi.org/10.1007/s11187-020-00316-0

Cattell, R. B. (1966). The scree test for the number of factors. *Multivariate Behavioral Research, 1*(2), 245–276.

Chembessi, C., Bourdin, S., & Torre, A. (2024). Towards a territorialisation of the circular economy: The proximity of stakeholders and resources matters. *Cambridge Journal of Regions, Economy and Society, 17*(3), 605–622.

Coenen, L., & Truffer, B. (2012). Places and spaces of sustainability transitions: Geographical contributions to an emerging research and policy field. *European Planning Studies, 20*(3), 367–374.

Colombelli, A., Paolucci, E., & Ughetto, E. (2019). Hierarchical and relational governance and the life cycle of entrepreneurial ecosystems. *Small Business Economics, 52*, 505–521.

Debizet, G., Pappalardo, M., & Wurtz, F. (2022). *Local energy communities: Emergence, places, organizations, decision tools*. Taylor & Francis.

Deutz, P., Jonas, A. E., Newsholme, A., Pusz, M., Rogers, H. A., Affolderbach, J., Baumgartner, R. J., & Ramos, T. B. (2024). The role of place in the development of a circular economy: A critical analysis of potential for social redistribution in Hull, UK. *Cambridge Journal of Regions, Economy and Society, 17*(3), 551–564.

Dragan, D. (2020). Legal barriers to the development of energy clusters in Poland. *European Energy and Environmental Law Review, 29*(1), 14–20.

Dreyfus, M., & Suwa, A. (2022). *Local energy governance: Opportunities and challenges for renewable and decentralised energy in France and Japan*. Routledge.

European Parliament. (2012, July 4). *Regulation (EU) No 648/2012 of the European Parliament and of the Council of July 4, 2012 on OTC derivatives, central counterparties and trade repositories*. European Parliament. http://data.europa.eu/eli/reg/2012/648

European Parliament. (2018). *Directive (EU) 2018/2001 of the European Parliament and of the Council of December 11, 2018 on the promotion of the use of energy from renewable sources (recast)*. European Parliament. http://data.europa.eu/eli/dir/2018/2001

European Parliament. (2019, June 5). *Directive (EU) 2019/944 of the European Parliament and of the Council of June 5, 2019 on common rules for the internal market for electricity and amending Directive 2012/27/EU (recast)*. European Parliament. http://data.europa.eu/eli/dir/2019/944

Gancarczyk, M., & Gancarczyk, J. (2013). Structural change in industrial clusters–scenarios and policy implications. *Studia Regionalia*, *35*, 111–127.

Gancarczyk, M., Gancarczyk, J., & Reichel, M. (2024). Revitalizing forgotten spaces through local leadership and social entrepreneurial ecosystems: The case of Muszyna commune. In M. del Carmen Sánchez-Carreira, P. J. R. Mourão, & B. Blanco-Varela (Eds.), *European regional policy and development* (pp. 105–134). Routledge.

Gancarczyk, M., & Ujwary-Gil, A. (2020). *Revitalizing industrial policy through smart, micro-level and bottom-up approaches*. In A. Ujwary-Gil, & M. Gancarczyk (Eds.), *New challenges in economic policy, business and management* (pp. 11–29). Polish Academy of Sciences.

Gancarczyk, M., Ujwary-Gil, A., & González-López, M. (2021). The expansion of the smart specialization concept and practice. In M. Gancarczyk, A. Ujwary-Gil, & M. González-López (Eds.), *Partnerships for regional innovation and development* (pp. 1–18). Routledge.

Grillitsch, M. (2015). Institutional layers, connectedness and change: Implications for economic evolution in regions. *European Planning Studies*, *23*(10), 2099–2124.

Gryszczuk A. (2024, January 15). *Zmiany w prawie dla klastrów energii. Czego zabrakło? (Changes in the law for energy clusters. What is missing?)* [Interview]. https://www.gramwzielone.pl/trendy/20178467/zmiany-w-prawie-dla-klastrow-energii-czego-zabraklo

Hassink, R. (2019). How to decontextualize in economic geography? *Dialogues in Human Geography*, *9*(3), 279–282.

Kuźniacki, A., & Borek, B. (2023). Klastry energii jako niezbędny e element zmian modelu polskiej energetyki. *Nowa Energia*, 78–81.

Lowitzsch, J., Hoicka, C. E., & van Tulder, F. J. (2020). Renewable energy communities under the 2019 European clean energy package – Governance model for the energy clusters of the future? *Renewable and Sustainable Energy Reviews*, *122*. https://doi.org/10.1016/j.rser.2019.109489

Luken, R., & Castellanos-Silveria, F. (2011). Industrial transformation and sustainable development in developing countries. *Sustainable Development*, *19*(3), 167–175.

Mataczyńska, E., & Kucharska, A. (Eds.) (2020). *Energy clusters: Regulation, theory and practice. I*. Łukasiewicz Institute of Energy Policy.

Micek, D., Kocór, M., Worek, B., & Szczucka, A. (2021). *Społeczne uwarunkowania funkcjonowania klastrów energii w Polsce: Raport podsumowujący analizę studium przypadku wybranych klastrów: Cz. 3*. Ministerstwo Rozwoju, Pracy i Technologii, Akademia Górniczo-Hutnicza im. Stanisława Staszica w Krakowie, Narodowe Centrum Badań Jądrowych. https://www.er.agh.edu.pl/media/filer_public/66/cb/66cb3fd2-854d-47c5-baaa-c2952fb8e639/raport_spoleczne_uwarunkowania_funkcjonowania_klastrow_energii_w_polsce.pdf

Nadeem, T. B., Siddiqui, M., Khalid, M., & Asif, M. (2023). Distributed energy systems: A review of classification, technologies, applications, and policies. *Energy Strategy Reviews*, *48*, 101096.

O'Connor, A., Stam, E., Sussan, F., & Audretsch, D. B. (2018). Entrepreneurial ecosystems: The foundations of place-based renewal. In A. O'Connor, E. Stam, F. Sussan, & D. Audretsch (Eds.), *Entrepreneurial ecosystems: Place-based transformations and transitions* (pp. 1–21). Springer.

Ostrom, E. (1986). An agenda for the study of institutions. *Public Choice*, *48*(1), 3–25.

Schwabe, J. (2024). Regime-driven niches and institutional entrepreneurs: Adding hydrogen to regional energy systems in Germany. *Energy Research & Social Science*, *108*, 103357.

Shakib, M. D. (2020). Using system dynamics to evaluate policies for industrial clusters development. *Computers & Industrial Engineering*, *147*, 106637.

Speck, S., Paleari, S., Tagliapietra, S., & Zoboli, R. (2023). *Investments in the sustainability transition: Leveraging green industrial policy against emerging constraints*. EEA European Environment Agency. https://doi.org/10.2800/451268

Surwillo, I. (2022). Energy clusters in Poland: Towards diffused green energy communities. In F. Karimi, & M. Rodi (Eds.), *Energy transition in the Baltic Sea Region* (pp. 185–204). Routledge.

Tałan, K. (2021). The distributed energy sector in Poland: Current status, challenges, barriers, and the Danish experience. *Energy Policy Studies*, *1*(7), 12–26.

Trejo-Nieto, A. (2021). Green industrial policies for sustainability and resilience. In R. Brears (Ed.), *The Palgrave encyclopedia of sustainable resources and ecosystem resilience* (pp. 1–18). Springer International Publishing. https://doi.org/10.1007/978-3-030-67776-3_33-1

Williamson, O. E. (2000). The new institutional economics: Taking stock, looking ahead. *Journal of Economic Literature*, *38*(3), 595–613.

Zukauskaite, E., Trippl, M., & Plechero, M. (2017). Institutional thickness revisited. *Economic Geography*, *93*(4), 325–345.

Conclusion

This monograph has accomplished the objective to conceptualize the role of energy cluster policies in sustainable industrial transformation (SIT) using an institutional approach, as well as to identify the progress of the energy cluster policies and the development stages, drivers, and obstacles of local energy clusters. *The major contribution from our research* is a development and empirical corroboration of a research framework for evaluating the advancement of policies for energy-sustainable industrial transformation (ESIT) through cluster initiatives. This work elucidates the causal interconnections between institutional configurations and the development of energy clusters and their progression in ESIT (Acemoglu et al., 2002; Benner, 2021; Gancarczyk et al., 2023; Ostrom, 1986; Williamson, 2000). Based on this framework, we identify and explain the advancement of policies for energy cluster initiatives, as well as the development stages, drivers and obstacles of local energy clusters. Moreover, the referred conceptual advancement can serve as an analytical framework for policy evaluations in other country contexts. *The general argument* of the adopted conceptual lens is that the progress in policies for ESIT through cluster initiatives can be understood and evaluated by recognizing institutional arrangements. This includes local socioeconomic governance within cluster initiatives, as well as national and international legislation and policies.

The overarching objective of the monograph was approached on both conceptual and empirical bases. Specifically, it was prefaced by the accomplishment of the following detailed objectives: i) identifying the advancement of energy cluster policies in Poland considering a multiscalar context at the local, regional, country, and international levels; ii) identifying the development phases and types of energy cluster initiatives in Poland; iii) identifying the barriers and drivers of energy cluster initiatives in Poland; and iv) synthesizing the recommendations for energy cluster policies to enhance sustainable industrial transformation.

Our research addressed Research Question 1 by analyzing Polish cluster policies' development phases at local, national, and international levels. We identified socioeconomic governance characteristics based

DOI: 10.4324/9781003623540-6

on cluster policy literature. The energy cluster policies are at an early stage. From 2015 to 2024, national legislatures introduced new membership provisions, cluster agreements, reporting, and official registration. Regulations improved fee conditions related to renewable energy sources adoption and energy self-sufficiency. However, there are controversies over narrowing membership, lacking incentives for diverse participation, and neglecting governance practices. Ambiguity regarding energy clusters' purpose hinders policy adjustments. Drawing from international experiences since the 1980s, Polish policies are evolving and should adapt to international frameworks and best practices. Regional policies should serve as complementary growth incentives considering the cluster initiatives' spatial nature.

In response to Research Question 2, we identified two phases in Poland's energy cluster initiatives for sustainable industrial transformation: birth and intermediate phases. They differ in governance characteristics and ESIT indicators. Governance, ESIT effects, and capability properties offer a detailed profile of the groups' structural features.

The barriers and drivers of energy cluster initiatives in Poland were described, answering the Research Question 3. The study identified energy cluster profiles that can inform policies by aligning them with theoretical governance and policy objectives for ESIT advancement. These profiles were enhanced with evaluations of key obstacles and development drivers, along with suggested solutions from respondents. A fundamental conclusion drawn from these detailed analyses is that clusters at various stages of development exhibit certain shared requirements, notably concerning legal facilitators. Clusters in their initial stages of development encounter deficiencies in capital, infrastructure, and coordination with energy operators, encapsulated as financial and capital shortfalls as well as elevated transaction costs. The progression of emerging clusters is contingent upon appropriate access to financial capital and their integration into the system, necessitating a reduction in transaction costs, including distribution fees and negotiations with operators. Clusters in the intermediate phase encounter equivalent barriers, while also underscoring supplementary challenges critical for local energy provision, efficiency, and safety. These challenges and drivers are pivotal for industrial policy, concentrating on upgrading, competitiveness, and advancement. Moreover, clusters also necessitate policy strategies that are appropriately aligned with their specific profiles (Benner, 2021; Colombelli et al., 2019).

Research Question 4 sought recommendations for energy cluster policies to enhance sustainable industrial transformation. We recommend a granular approach to policy evaluations, focusing on evolutionary processes and development phases. Policies should match the identified barriers and drivers to these development phases. Regional and national policy levels should learn from local industrial relations, and agencies should adapt international good practices to their contexts.

The monograph fills in the research gaps. *First, our research fills the gap in context-dependent studies to improve the design of place-based energy policies* (Coenen & Truffer, 2012; Luken & Castellanos-Silveria, 2011; Smith et al., 2004). We have demonstrated that a detailed approach to cluster development serves to identify impediments and catalysts for growth, offering policy recommendations (Ashford et al., 2002; Chembessi et al., 2024; Coenen & Truffer, 2012). This study underscores the significance of institutional elements, specifically the governance in the provision of local energy, while recognizing multiscalar contexts including international and national legislative and policy frameworks. Although grounded in specific contexts, it provides an analytical framework that can inform research and policy formation in other environments. Moreover, it contributes to the understanding of the initial and intermediate phases of sustainability within the energy sectors of Central and Eastern Europe (Dragan, 2020; Grigore & Dragan, 2020; Micek et al., 2021; Mirowski & Kubica, 2016; Surwillo, 2022).

Second, this research addresses the knowledge gap in the conceptual background for energy-focused SIT and identifies the policy arrangements that favor or impede this transition (Bohatkiewicz-Czaicka & Gancarczyk, 2025; Micek et al., 2021; Surwillo, 2022). A theoretical approach is adopted, with a particular emphasis on the institutional and evolutionary dimensions of SIT. This approach has demonstrated to be a productive conceptual framework for formulating actionable recommendations concerning economic and legal interventions (Ashford et al., 2002; Grigore & Dragan, 2020; Smith et al., 2004). The institutional perspective and emphasis on socioeconomic governance remain less explored in comparison to the technical and legal aspects of governance within the context of energy transition (Luken & Castellanos-Silveria, 2011; Smith et al., 2004; Speck et al., 2023; Trejo-Nieto, 2021).

Third, we addressed the research gap of predominant qualitative case studies in the area of energy transitions (Afeltowicz et al., 2024; Micek et al., 2021; Surwillo, 2022). Employing a representative sample of energy clusters initiatives alongside quantitative statistical methods, our research offers a more robust generalization compared to the analytical generalization derived primarily from case-based investigations.

Our work contributes to the current research on energy clusters, cluster-based policies and sustainable industrial transformation. It developed an analytical framework for cluster policies in the area of ESIT. Our research delineates the conditions necessary for a local-level green transition, which are imperative for implementing place-based policies that can stimulate local energy clusters and can be replicated in other regions to establish distributed energy systems (Dreyfus & Suwa, 2022). The merit of this approach is rooted in its ability to enhance energy management and grid resilience, while also structuring adaptable frameworks that support sustainable transitions across diverse regions (Hassink, 2019). Recommendations for energy cluster policies were formulated, with a foundation grounded in European Union (EU) energy, cluster-based, and sustainable development policies. Comprehending the development phase, growth conditions, and policy measures pertinent to cluster-based SIT remains instrumental for cluster administration and policymakers. The principal recommendations emphasized the integration of clusters within the prevailing energy infrastructure, the establishment of legal incentives for the comprehensive representation of stakeholders within a cluster, and a call for increased public and private sector investment in technological and business model innovations to advance energy transitions.

References

Acemoglu, D., Johnson, S., & Robinson, J. A. (2002). Reversal of fortune: Geography and institutions in the making of the modern world income distribution. *The Quarterly Journal of Economics*, *117*(4), 1231–1294.

Afeltowicz, Ł., Nawojczyk, M., & Tyrała, R. (2024). Entrepreneurial actions in energy transition: A study of three local energy clusters in Poland. *European Urban and Regional Studies*, *31*(2), 132–148. https://doi.org/10.1177/09697764231179667

Ashford, N. A., Hafkamp, W., Prakke, F., & Vergragt, P. (2002). *Pathways to Sustainable Industrial Transformations: Co-optimising Competitiveness, Employment, and Environment*. In *Conference engineering education in sustainable development* (pp. 582–601). https://research.tudelft.nl/en/publications/pathways-to-sustainable-industrial-transformations-co-optimising-

Benner, M. (2021). Retheorizing industrial–institutional coevolution: A multidimensional perspective. *Regional Studies*, *56*(3), 1–14

Bohatkiewicz-Czaicka, J., & Gancarczyk, M. (2025). *Industrial clusters in international value chains: Conceptual advancement and empirical evidence from European ICT clusters*. Taylor & Francis.

Chembessi, C., Bourdin, S., & Torre, A. (2024). Towards a territorialisation of the circular economy: The proximity of stakeholders and resources matters. *Cambridge Journal of Regions, Economy and Society*, *17*(3), 605–622.

Coenen, L., & Truffer, B. (2012). Places and spaces of sustainability transitions: Geographical contributions to an emerging research and policy field. *European Planning Studies*, *20*(3), 367–374.

Colombelli, A., Paolucci, E., & Ughetto, E. (2019). Hierarchical and relational governance and the life cycle of entrepreneurial ecosystems. *Small Business Economics*, *52*(2), 505–521. https://doi.org/10.1007/s11187-017-9957-4

Dragan, D. (2020). Legal barriers to the development of energy clusters in Poland. *European Energy and Environmental Law Review*, *29*(1), 14–20.

Dreyfus, M., & Suwa, A. (2022). *Local energy governance: Opportunities and challenges for renewable and decentralised energy in France and Japan*. Taylor & Francis.

Gancarczyk, M., Najda-Janoszka, M., Gancarczyk, J., & Hassink, R. (2023). Exploring regional innovation policies and regional industrial transformation from a coevolutionary perspective: The case of Małopolska, Poland. *Economic Geography*, *99*(1), 51–80. https://doi.org/10.1080/00130095.2022.2120465

Grigore, A. M., & Dragan, I. M. (2020). Towards sustainable entrepreneurial ecosystems in a transitional economy: An analysis of two Romanian city-regions through the lens of entrepreneurs. *Sustainability (Switzerland)*, *12*(15). https://doi.org/10.3390/su12156061

Hassink, R. (2019). How to decontextualize in economic geography? *Dialogues in Human Geography*, *9*(3), 279–282.

Luken, R., & Castellanos-Silveria, F. (2011). Industrial transformation and sustainable development in developing countries. *Sustainable Development*, *19*(3), 167–175.

Micek, D., Kocór, M., Worek, B., & Szczucka, A. (2021). *Społeczne uwarunkowania funkcjonowania klastrów energii w Polsce: Raport podsumowujący analizę studium przypadku wybranych klastrów: Cz. 3*. Ministerstwo Rozwoju, Pracy i Technologii, Akademia Górniczo-Hutnicza im. Stanisława Staszica w Krakowie, Narodowe Centrum Badań Jądrowych. https://www.er.agh.edu.pl/media/filer_public/66/cb/66cb3fd2-854d-47c5-baaa-c2952fb8e639/raport_spoleczne_uwarunkowania_funkcjonowania_klastrow_energii_w_polsce.pdf

Mirowski, T., & Kubica, K. (2016). The role of biomass in energy clusters. *Polityka Energetyczna*, *19*(4), 125–138.

Ostrom, E. (1986). An agenda for the study of institutions. *Public Choice*, *48*(1), 3–25.

Smith, A., Stirling, A., & Berkhout, F. (2004). *Governing sustainable industrial transformation under different transition contexts*. In *Governance for Industrial Transformation, Proceedings of the 2003 Berlin Conference on the Human Dimensions of Global Environmental Change* (pp. 113–132). https://www.academia.edu/download/30715730/10.1.1.197.8530.pdf

Speck, S., Paleari, S., Tagliapietra, S., & Zoboli, R. (2023). *Investments in the sustainability transition: Leveraging green industrial policy against emerging constraints*. EEA European Environment Agency. https://doi.org/10.2800/451268

Surwillo, I. (2022). Energy clusters in Poland: Towards diffused green energy communities. In F. Karimi, & M. Rodi (Eds.), *Energy transition in the Baltic Sea region* (pp. 185–204). Routledge.

Trejo-Nieto, A. (2021). Green industrial policies for sustainability and resilience. In R. Brears (Ed.), *The Palgrave encyclopedia of sustainable resources and ecosystem resilience* (pp. 1–18). Springer International Publishing. https://doi.org/10.1007/978-3-030-67776-3_33-1

Williamson, O. E. (2000). The new institutional economics: Taking stock, looking ahead. *Journal of Economic Literature*, *38*(3), 595–613.

Index

Note: *Italicized* and **bold** page numbers refer to figures and tables.

access to finance 98–99

captive coordination 18
CC *see* Cluster Coordinator (CC)
Cluster Coordinator (CC) 63–65
cluster development: institutional approach to 23–24; paths 24–25; stages and determinants of 25–27
cluster initiatives 2–5, 15, 20, 37, 41, 46, 49, 53, 58–59, *59*, 61–65, **84**, 89, 94, **94**, *95*, **95**, *96*, 98–100, 103–107, 113, 114; in distributed energy system and specificity 100–102
cluster organization 20, 37, 48, 51, 93, 95, 98
cluster policy 40–41, 57–75; data sources 61–65; fragmentation of 41; measurement of variables 69–72, **70–71**, **72**; methods and analytical techniques 60–61, **61**; research framework variables, operationalization 66–69, **67–68**; research procedure 65; research sample, characteristics of 73–75, **74**
clusters: characteristics of 16; as cooperative network structures 19–21; development *see* cluster development; energy *see* energy clusters; evolution of 19; governance of 17–19, 58, 59, 66, 69, **72**; grid-based 101, 102; in industrial transitions, significance of 21; initiatives *see* cluster initiatives; as institutional structures 15–21; organization of 20; policy *see* cluster policy; virtual 101–103
coevolution 3–5, 11, 13–14, 21, 22, 60, 66

deductive mixed-method approach 4
direct public support 98–99
distributed energy 44–46, 98, 103, 104, 108, 115; system, specificity and purpose of energy cluster initiatives in 100–102

EE *see* entrepreneurial ecosystem (EE)
energy clusters 36–53; contract agreements 51, **52**; coordinator, role of 51–52; definition of 2, 36–37; developmental phases of 81–88, *82*, **83–86**, **88**; in energy policy directions 43–44; in European Union legislation 38, 40; in European Union policy directions 42; as foundation for achieving sustainable development policy 46–48, **48**; funding for 51; institutional framework for 49–53; in Polish legislation 38, **39**; in Polish policy directions 41–43; properties of 36–37; in regional policy directions 42–43; sustainable industrial transformation in 81–110
energy communities 4, 37, 41, 45–48, 100, 101, 103, 105, 109
energy industry 2, 11, 59, 69, 83, 100, 107
energy policy directions, energy clusters in 43–44
Energy Regulatory Office 49, 100
energy sector 6, 49, 50, 115
energy-sustainable industrial transformation (ESIT) 3, 5, 57–58, 61, 81, 83, 84, 93, 106, 113, 114; advancement of policies for *59*; measurement of variables 66, **67**, 69,

70; scale reliability for **72**; *see also* sustainable industrial transformation (SIT)
entrepreneurial ecosystem (EE) 21, 25, 26, 88, 92
environmental policy 62
ERDF *see* European Regional Development Fund (ERDF)
ESF *see* European Social Fund (ESF)
ESIT *see* energy-sustainable industrial transformation (ESIT)
Europe 2020: A strategy for smart, sustainable, and inclusive growth 41
European Commission 40–42
European Green Deal 1, 44
European Regional Development Fund (ERDF) 51
European Social Fund (ESF) 51
European Union legislation, energy clusters in 38, 40; policy directions 42
evolutionary approach 14, 23–27, 60, 104, 107

"Fit for 55" package 44
Fourth Industrial Revolution 12

GDP *see* gross domestic product (GDP)
General Assembly of the UN 46
globalization 24
governance: cluster 17–19, 58, 59, 66, 69, **72**; of distributed energy 104; institutional 26

Human Capital Operational Program 51

IEP *see* installed energy power (IEP)
Industrial Development Agency 49
industrial policy 6, 12–13, 22, 25, 40, 98, 102, 105–107, 109, 114
industrial transformation: regional 5, 23–25, 69; sustainable *see* sustainable industrial transformation (SIT)
Industry 4.0 12
Innovative Economy Operational Program 51
installed energy power (IEP) 91
institutional embeddedness 17
institutional governance 26
institutional perspective 11–27; clusters *see* clusters; coevolutionary approach 13–14, 22; foundations 11–12; paradigm 22–23; policies 12–13
intermediary institutions 17

Just Transition Fund 45, 51

lead tenants, roles of 99–100

membership, structure of 99–100
Ministry for Climate and Environment 49
Ministry of Development and Technology 49
Ministry of Economy 49
Ministry of Energy 49
Ministry of Science and Higher Education 49
multiscalarity 14

National Chamber of Energy Clusters (NCEC) 63–65, 103
National Energy Conservation Agency 37
National Institute for Distributed Energy 37
NCEC *see* National Chamber of Energy Clusters (NCEC)
network linkages 19
New Industrial Policy (NIP) 12, 13, 22, 63, 98, 101
New Industrial Strategy for Europe 13
New Institutional Economics 66
NIP *see* New Industrial Policy (NIP)

Our common future 45–46

Paris Agreement 45
path branching 25
path creation 25
path exhaustion 25
path trajectories 24, 25
place-based approach 57, 60, 63, 115
Poland's Strategy for Responsible Development 45
policy formulation 12–13
Polish Agency for Enterprise Development 49
Polish Council of Ministers 44
Polish Energy Policy until 2040 50
Polish legislation, energy clusters in 38, **39**; policy directions 41–43
public governance, comprehensive view of 104
public-private partnership, energy clusters as 38

Recovery and Resilience Facility (RRF): National Recovery and Resilience Plan 51
Recovery Plan for Europe 51
regional innovation systems 21
Regional Operational Programs 51
regional industrial transformation 5, 23–25, 69
regional policy directions, energy clusters in 42–43
relational coordination 18
renewable energy sources (RESs) 14, 40, 44, 49, 50, 59, 73–75, 86–87, 89, 91–93, 96, 98, 100–103, 110
Renewable Energy Sources Act: Article 184k 50
RES Act 52
Responsible Development Strategy 44
RESs *see* renewable energy sources (RESs)
RRF *see* Recovery and Resilience Facility (RRF)

SDGs *see* Sustainable Development Goals (SDGs)
SIT *see* sustainable industrial transformation (SIT)
spatial proximity 14, 15, 44, 105
Statistics Poland 45
sustainability 17, 48, 57, 69, 104, 115
Sustainable Development Goals (SDGs) 46
sustainable development policy: energy clusters as foundation for achieving 46–48, **48**; essence of 45–46; local energy communities in 45–48
sustainable industrial transformation (SIT) 1, 3, 5, 6, 23, 81–110, 113, 115, 116; benchmarks of 105; country- and regional-level institutions as enablers of energy cluster development, importance of 104–105; developmental phases of 81–88, *82*, **83–86**, **88**; distributed energy system, specificity and purpose of energy cluster initiatives in 100–102; economic policy, recommendations for 98–105; energy cluster groups against resource and capability potential, characteristics of 89–93, **89**, *90*, **92**; energy clusters as recognized parties in economic system and energy provision 103; energy clusters in intermediate and birth development phases, barriers and drivers of 93–98, **94**, *95*, **95**, *96*, **97**; future research directions of 107–110; good practice 105; industrial relations in energy system, structuring and clarifying 102–103; institutional approach to 11–27; limitations of 107–110; policies and related support instruments, tailoring 104; public governance, comprehensive view of 104; *see also* energy-sustainable industrial transformation (ESIT)

For Product Safety Concerns and Information please contact our EU representative GPSR@taylorandfrancis.com
Taylor & Francis Verlag GmbH, Kaufingerstraße 24, 80331 München, Germany

www.ingramcontent.com/pod-product-compliance
Lightning Source LLC
LaVergne TN
LVHW010930110826
845149LV00013B/2534

* 9 7 8 1 0 4 1 0 3 3 7 1 4 *